Competing Visions of Paradise

The Religious Contours of California
Window to the World's Religions

A nine-volume series co-edited by
Phillip E. Hammond and Ninian Smart
DEPARTMENT OF RELIGIOUS STUDIES
UNIVERSITY OF CALIFORNIA, SANTA BARBARA

VOLUME I
Californian Catholicism
KAY ALEXANDER

VOLUME II
Pilgrim Progression: *The Protestant Experience in California*
ELDON G. ERNST AND DOUGLAS FIRTH ANDERSON

VOLUME III
Competing Visions of Paradise:
The California Experience of 19th Century American Sectarianism
JOHN K. SIMMONS AND BRIAN WILSON

VOLUME IV
Diaspora in a Golden Land:
The Judaisms of California
RICHARD D. HECHT,
WITH RICHARD L. HOCH AND AVA G. KAHN

FORTHCOMING BOOKS ON:
Native American Religions
East Asian Religions
Islam
New Religious Movements
South Asian Religions

Competing Visions of Paradise

The California Experience of 19th Century American Sectarianism

JOHN K. SIMMONS
and BRIAN WILSON

VOLUME III OF
The Religious Contours of California
Window to the World's Religions

A PROJECT OF
The Center for the Study of Religion
University of California, Santa Barbara

IN ASSOCIATION WITH
The California Historical Society

FITHIAN PRESS
SANTA BARBARA • 1993

BR
555
.C2
S56
1993

Design and typography by Jim Cook

Published by Fithian Press
Post Office Box 1525
Santa Barbara, California 93102

LIBRARY OF CONGRESS CATALOGING-IN-PUBLICATION DATA
Simmons, John.
    Competing visions of Paradise: the California experience of 19th-century American sectarianism / John Simmons & Brian Wilson.
        p. cm. — (The Religious contours of California: v. 3)
    Includes bibliographical references and index.
    ISBN 1-56474-064-1
    1. Christian sects—California—History—19th century.
2. California—Church history. I. Wilson, Brian. II. Title. III. Series.
BR555.C2S56   1993
280'.4'09794—dc20
                                                    93-14259
                                                        CIP

Contents

The Religious Contours
of California

The series of books of which this volume is part is meant to engage the interest of California's citizens in the religions of their state. These range from Christian groups to Muslims, from Jews to Buddhists. They include the religions of Native Americans, of East Asian immigrants, and varieties of African American faith. The "new" religious movements of the 1960s and '70s are well represented in this state, as well as religions born in nineteenth-century America, such as Mormonism and Christian Science, and they too are part of this series. California, as is well known, is a heterogeneous society, and its religious life is likewise diverse; our series reveals just how diverse.

The series has a second purpose, however, and that is to inform readers about the world's religions. It is one thing to learn, for example, about Islam, Judaism, or Christianity as they have been and are practiced in California; it is another thing to discover where such religions originated, how they developed, and where else they currently are found. Each volume in the series therefore fits, at least loosely, a common outline. Each begins with an introduction to some religious tradition as it is found in California, then moves to an analysis of the interplay of that tradition and the state: how is California affected by the presence of this tradition, and how is the tradition affected by its presence in California? It is during this analysis that the reader learns about the history and global experience of the religious tradition that is the book's focus, for in attempting to understand any spiritual tradition in California one necessarily compares the situation here with situations elsewhere. The series will be successful, then, to the degree readers find they have learned not only about a religion close at hand, but learned also about that religion worldwide.

The series arose out of a project pioneered at the University of California at Santa Barbara to help high school teachers and others understand world religions through their manifestations in California. We conceived the parallel idea of recruiting a team of authors who would be able to put together a lucid set of books to inform the general public of the ways in which this state has drawn on divergent sources of religious belief and practice in forming a multicultural and rich society. In many ways California is indeed the future.

We believe that this series will help to fulfill one of the obligations of the University of California: to bring knowledge and understanding to the citizens of this great state, and to others in America, and to return directly some of the benefits conferred on us as researchers and teachers by its tax-paying citizens. Thus, royalties from the sales of these books go not to the authors or editors but into a fund the purpose of which is the furtherance of the public's understanding of all religious traditions. We hope we can in such a way make a small contribution to a fruitful living together of diverse spiritual practices.

In all this we try to be what may be called warmly objective. The authors, as students of religion, wish to give a fair and rounded account of each religion. We are not, as scholars of religions, in the business of preaching, of course, but we wish to bring out something of the spirit of each tradition. This series is thus a contribution to the mutual understanding of religions as well as a means of giving readers an idea of California's religious variety. We are grateful to the Lilly Endowment and to the Provost at UCSB for their financial assistance in publishing the series.

PHILLIP E. HAMMOND
NINIAN SMART
Editors

1 A New Order of Things: California Dreaming

On the back of the common American one dollar bill, beneath the pyramid topped by a single staring eye, we find the Latin phrase *novus ordo seclorum*—in English, "a new order of things." In that simple phrase we can detect much of the impulse, the energy, the imagination that went into the creation of a new nation—the United States—the settling of the West including California, and, above all, the founding of uniquely American sectarian religious movements that sought to define this "new order of things" in ways that both reflected and transcended the cultural vision that sparked this grand human drama.

When we refer to nineteenth- and early twentieth-century *sectarian* religions, we are talking about religious groups that bear the "made-in-America" stamp: Mormonism, Adventism (including Seventh-Day Adventists and Jehovah's Witnesses), Christian Science, New Thought groups, and Pentecostalism. (We will define the terms "sectarian" and "sect" in a moment.) Most religious organizations that you might be able to identify arrived on this continent in the hearts and souls of believers who came from someplace else. For instance, French, Irish, Italians, and Hispanic immigrants brought Roman Catholicism; English, Scottish, Dutch, and German believers built a wide variety of Protestant Christian churches representing Methodism, Presbyterianism, Lutheranism,

Baptist groups, and others; over time, people from Asia or the Middle East carried Buddhism, Hinduism, Chinese religions, and Islam to the shores of America; settlers from Eastern European countries practiced Orthodox Christianity. Jews have been in North America since colonial times and have continued to migrate in small but significant numbers from the four corners of the world.

However small in numbers compared to immigrant religious organizations, our made-in-America sectarian groups have something very special and important to tell us about "the new order of things" that is California. In many ways, California has always been a vibrant microcosm of the entire nation; it is as though California provided a reservoir for all the zeal and zest that flowed across the United States as the continent was permanently transformed by frontier dreamers, schemers, and builders. Today, as it was in the mid-nineteenth century, the Golden State, despite all the cultural challenges she faces, is still seen as the land of endless possibility; the place where dreams come true. For the fervent believers in our made-in-America religions, California represented a kind of paradise where the religious perfection they sought could more easily be realized. Certainly, as we shall see, almost all of these religious groups quickly gained a foothold in the sundrenched cultural environment of California.

In this volume of the *Religious Contours of California: Window to the World's Religions* series, we will be exploring each of the above religions; in general, we will focus on the who, what, when, where, and how of each group as it emerges and grows in American society. Specifically, we will try to determine each group's place in the religious history of California as we develop some understanding of how the Golden State, for good or ill, affected the "new order of things" as envisioned by these believers.

In our quest to discover how these religious organizations went about seeking "perfection in paradise" in California, we will break down each investigation into five study areas: Prophet, Promise, Plan, Possibility, and Place.

Prophet

In the world of religion, where does the idea for a "new order of things" come from? Many religions claim that the inspiration to redefine the meaning of human life and recreate human culture comes through divine revelation. Others say the call emerges from the purified vision of some spiritually evolved human being. Whatever the source may be, we know that the beginnings of all new religious movements require a prophet; a leader who is able to articulate his or her vision in a way that captures the imagination of other human beings and sets them on the path towards remaking the world.

Often prophets are described as *charismatic* leaders in that the power and intensity of their teaching attracts people like iron filings to a magnet. Once attracted these fervent believers radically transform themselves and, as much as possible, society according to the prophet's call for a "new order of things." Prophets tend to be religiously minded people who find themselves at odds with the established religious institutions of their time. Understandably, the process of challenging a pervasive view of nature and the meaning of life can lead to enormous tension in society and even persecution of those who advocate a "new order of things."

In this volume, we will meet some of America's greatest, most controversial, yet most interesting prophets; the visionaries whose spiritual inspiration resulted in the institutional birth of nineteenth- and twentieth-century sectarian groups: Joseph Smith (Mormonism), William Miller and Ellen G. White (Adventism), Charles Taze Russell (Jehovah's Witnesses), Mary Baker Eddy (Christian Science), Emma Curtis Hopkins, Annie Rix Militz, Malinda Cramer, the Brooks sisters (New Thought groups), Andrew Jackson Davis and Thomas Lake Harris (Spiritualism), and Charles Parham and William Seymour (Pentecostalism). Though the "new order of things" described by these men and women often differs, we will discover certain similarities that link these made-in-America religions to central themes in our culture. And, though only a few of these religious leaders ever touched California soil, their religions found a home in the Golden State.

Promise

Having met our prophets, we will want to explore what, exactly, it was they envisioned. What did they promise their believers that, in each case, prompted such zealous reaction? What did they teach? For instance, the first group we will be investigating is the Mormons. There is, perhaps, no greater religious drama in the history of the United States than is found in the Mormon saga. Almost from the moment that the prophet Joseph Smith proclaimed his vision of a restored Christianity on the North American continent, he and his ever-growing group endured constant harassment. They were run out of New York state, then Kirkland, Ohio.

Seeking solitude, a peaceful oasis where they might freely practice their religion, they moved to Missouri only to encounter armed resistance to their presence. Many died in what came to be called the "Mormon wars." Hostility drove them back across the Mississippi River to Illinois, where, after building the largest city in the state at that time, Nauvoo, Joseph Smith was brutally murdered while being held in the Carthage jail. Yet again, Mormon men and women headed west, crossing the frozen Mississippi to begin their famous trek, under Brigham Young, towards a home in what is now Utah. In January of 1847, the first Mormon colonizers had entered California.

The point is that being a Mormon in the nineteenth century meant being persecuted. And yet the religion never stopped growing and the believers never gave up the struggle to see Joseph Smith's promise realized in the world around them. Today, Mormonism is one of the fastest growing religious organizations in the world!

It may be helpful, here, to make a comment about the power and pervasiveness of the religious promise in general. Religion is more than what goes on in those unusually shaped buildings that occupy prime real estate in the towns and cities of the world. It is more than just Judaism and Christianity or what is taught and learned by rote in the Sunday schools of America. Religion is a constant in life that provides human beings with meaning and purpose as it guides human activity. Even people who claim to have no religion, or describe themselves as atheists, must have some meaning system—a worldview—that orients them to the surrounding world.

The question of whether or not a person must have some kind of "religion" in order to function in life puts us into an interesting debate regarding the definition of religion—a debate we certainly do not need to go into at this point in our discussion. But many of us have experienced friends who have "given up" religion which, more accurately stated, is a rejection of the religious institution they were compelled to attend in their youth. Behind the usual vitriolic attack on religion, however, is a noticeable quest by these people to fill the void with something else; something that, for good or for ill, gives their life meaning and direction. It could be an obsession with fashion or a particular rock group, fanatic allegiance to a team in sports, or single-minded concentration on a career goal. It could be intoxicants and drug culture. Or, in time, they may come around passionately exclaiming how they have "found themselves" in a new religion. The fact is that human beings seek out models to guide their behavior; without them, the emotions of alienation, aloneness, and purposelessness often become overwhelming.

The point is that in each case, our made-in-America sectarian religions provided people with a new promise that seemed to lift believers out of their confusion and set them on a path towards mental, spiritual, and physical health. We can assume that the previous "religions" of these people simply were not doing the job in terms of answering life's challenges. Thus, in the nineteenth century, the promise of a "new order of things" attracted people who were searching beyond the boundaries of the established religions of the time.

Plan

This brings us nicely to our third study area and to some important considerations about what it means to be a "sectarian" religious movement. Prophets not only must make a promise to their people; they must provide a plan for carrying out that promise; a plan by which the "new order of things" may be realized. Joseph Smith had a plan for building Zion—or God's kingdom—on the North American continent. Mary Baker Eddy had a plan for overcoming the perceptual error of matter and spiritualizing the universe. Ellen G. White had a plan which called Adventists to prepare for the imminent return of Jesus Christ. Andrew Jackson Davis had a plan that allowed spiritualists to contact those who had passed on to other levels of consciousness. Parham and Seymour sought the Pentecostal "baptism by fire." In each of our sectarian religions, the plan required that adherents reorient themselves to the world and charge forward with renewed purpose towards a new destiny. Believers move from the "old order/old plan" to the "new order/new plan" with a sense of "born again" enthusiasm.

This transition from old to new is played out on the institutional level as the movement from an established religious *church* or *denomination* to a religious *sect*. Leaders of any religious organization like to give the impression that their belief systems and religious communities are rock solid and permanent. But the truth is that religious organizations always face challenges and undergo changes—the same challenges and changes that any type of institution in society faces. Over time, if the prophet's promise and plan are successfully realized, more people join the organization, the group may develop many different centers of worship, wealth must be distributed equitably, new and more grand buildings must be built, and the work to run all this institutional expansion becomes more weighty and complex. To put it simply, success brings complications.

In fact, the very success of a new religious movement as it grows into a bona fide religious organization generates a number of challenges that ultimately affect the group's stability. The first of these dilemmas might be called the "generation gap." The people who actually sat at the feet of the prophet made a conscious choice to change their lives by becoming part of the new order of things. But what of the next generation? What of the children born into the religion? Will they have the same enthusiasms? And, more importantly, will they have the same motivation to keep the "new order" on course?

A second dilemma: what happens when the prophet dies? The death of the charismatic leader creates at least two sub-problems: leadership and power. Who will lead the religious organization; will it be the son or daughter of the prophet; will it be a committee of the oldest living believers? How are the new leaders to be selected? Will the new leader or leaders be able to sustain the intensity of devotion in the rank-and-file believer? What may ensue is a power struggle for leadership that inevitably leaves some bad feelings among believers who are left out of the newly formulated avenues of power in the organization.

If the religious organization makes it through this crisis, other dilemmas rise up to challenge the group's stability. Again success brings complexity, and in any institution, this can result in the creation of an oppressive bureaucracy. For example, institutions of higher education are in a constant struggle between idealism and practicality. On the one hand, the educational goal is the creation and expression, through teaching, of knowledge. On the other hand, as an educational institution expands, *because it is successful in meeting these noble goals,* practical concerns loom large: new buildings must be built, salaries for distinguished faculty force tuition up, grant competitions for government funds cut into teaching time, and an expanded student body places additional administrative demands on the entire system. These bureaucratic challenges, and many others, complicate and vitiate against the once pristine focus on knowledge. Even at the most mundane levels, success can spoil perfection: the quiet "bed and breakfast" loses its ambiance as it succumbs to tourism; the serenity of a National Park is despoiled by the mob seeking a nature experience; the Beatles disband under the pressures of their '60s success, yet the Rolling Stones somehow struggle through the institutionalization of their once spontaneous musical charm. The list could go on and on.

Of course, when religious organizations become overly bureaucratic, the effect can be even more damaging. Religion is that aspect of human experience which is supposed to take you out of the ordinary and into the extraordinary. Whether it is a feeling of closeness to God, a mystical sense of oneness with the cosmos, or a meditative state of peace, human beings seek religious experience, among other reasons, for a release from the nagging trivialities of day-to-day living. But if life in the religious community revolves around committees on finance and building maintenance, election of members to run the organization, long-range planning, and other kinds of worldly ventures, the "religious" aspect of the undertaking begins to fade and members begin to look for something more spiritually authentic.

Yet another dilemma involves the maintenance of the vitality of the group's rituals and teachings (doctrines). A rather common declaration from the recently "de-churched" goes for something like, "I've stopped going to church. It's *so* boring!" Certainly if key prayers are "just words," hymns have bizarre melodies that are hard to sing, and there is no "meaning" to the ritual actions performed by the community of believers, the whole point of attending the church is lost. Again, we are speaking of the experiential dimension in religions. If nothing extraordinary happens at the religious service, a person will do one of two things: a) seek out a "new order of things," that is, look for religion that "works"; or, and this is more often the case, make a decision that "religion" is unreal or untrue and, thus, turn away from this remarkably creative expression of human culture and consciousness.

From a believer's perspective, the same kind of experiential demands are made on the religious organization's doctrines. Doctrines can both positively and negatively affect a group's stability. On one hand, doctrines are a necessity in that they define the system of belief that identifies the religion in question. For example, when a late night conversation turns to religion, it usually centers on the set of doctrines that comprise and delineate a particular faith.

On the other hand, what happens if those teachings no longer satisfy the very human need to have clear, understandable answers to life's profound questions: who am I; why am I here; what is the meaning of life; what is the purpose of living; where do I go when I die? Someone once described religious doctrines as the institutionalization of answers about the unexaminable and unexplainable. For instance, a standard Christian teaching regarding death is that good people go to heaven and bad people burn in hell. But scientists from NASA have never launched a space probe that has streaked past the planets, the Milky Way, the distant stars and sent back pictures of a place where people with wings sit on clouds and play harps. And no geological expedition has, as yet, discovered people with pointy ears, spiked tails, and cloven hoofs tormenting deceased humans in the molten lava of the earth's core.

In other words, we cannot prove these teachings through evidence provided by our senses of the methods of scientific investigation. We believe religious doctrines because we have *faith* in the authority of the religious institution that proclaims these teachings as universal "truths." But what happens if faith is lost in these doctrines and/or the authority of the church to which they belong? What if the doctrines of a believer's religion become just a collection of antiquated rules and regulations that no longer carry a sense of meaning or authority? A person might continue to attend church services simply for the sense of community; or maybe seek out a religious organization with more "believable" doctrines; or, if this believer has the makings of a prophet, she or he might redefine key teachings in a way that renews faith and attracts others to join a new order of things. In this last scenario, a *sect* is created.

Each of the made-in-America religions we will be exploring is a variety of Christian sect. Since the Protestant Reformation—a major cultural/historical event in the sixteenth century during which Christian believers seeking institutional and spiritual freedom broke off from the Roman Catholic church—Christianity has had a tendency to respond to organizational dilemmas in a sectar-

ian manner. In other words, if the type of Christianity being practiced has lost its spiritual "zip," people *will* follow a prophet with a
new or renewed Christian promise; a new sect is born. When the
ingredient of "religious freedom" is mixed in—one of our most
cherished rights protected by the Constitution of the United
States—the process becomes even more dramatic. In fact, it is estimated that there are over 900 different varieties of Christianity in
this country; proof of a vibrant, healthy *sectarian impulse* in the religious imagination of the American people.

Though it is certainly beyond the scope of this book to completely explain the organizational differences between a church, a
denomination, a sect, and a cult, we should at least be aware that
scholars, religious leaders, and believers do not always agree on
the definition of "sect" nor do they agree on how and when to
apply the term in describing a given religious group. For over a
hundred years, sociologists of religion have tried to hammer out
criteria for determining these types of religious organizations and
basically have come up with two major defining characteristics.
The first criterion concerns the level of *tension* between a particular
group and other social institutions in the dominant society. In
other words a church or denomination would more readily represent the values, culture, and traditions of the surrounding social
environment; tension, meaning anything from pejorative remarks
about the religion all the way to physical and legal attacks, would
be at a minimum. Because sects and cults *do* represent a "new
order of things," and may be at odds with established patterns of
behavior in society, it follows that there will be more tension, more
friction between these groups and other social institutions be they
political, legal, educational, or religious.

The second criterion focuses on the relationship the new group
has with its parent organization. According to this defining model,
a group that attempts to *renew* the "true faith" is a *sect*; a group that
in reality is completely breaking off from the cultural glacier of the
parent church and floating off into an ocean of *innovation* is termed
a *cult*. As you can imagine, believers who are left behind in the parent organization have a tendency to see no cultural connection
between their group and the "new order of things." At the same
time, adherents to the new faith see themselves as representatives
of the "truest expression" of the religion which the parent church is
guilty of corrupting.

For our purposes, this means that we will find many people defining our nineteenth- and twentieth-century religions as "cults" because, from their perspective, the "new order of things" envisioned in each case is simply too innovative to be considered Christian by the older Christian establishment. We will call them sects out of deference to the prophets and believers in each new religion who, to a person, saw themselves as bringing renewed Christianity back to the people.

Possibility

Returning again to our consideration of organizational dilemmas, it is clear that, in the world of religion, they contribute to what we have called the *sectarian impulse*. Success, for any religious organization, generates complexity; complexity inevitably creates dissatisfaction on the part of some believers; dissatisfaction, in turn, can lead to people leaving the religious organization to create a "new order of things." But not all attempts to establish a sect are successful. This brings us to our fourth study area: possibility. The possibility of the new sectarian movement being successful is dependent on a host of social, cultural, personal, political, geographical, even geological factors. As we explore our made-in-America sectarian movements, we find that these factors came together in such a way that, in each case, the fragile sectarian seed was able to blossom into a full-grown religious movement.

For example, Joseph Smith, our Mormon prophet, grew up in the early 1800s in a part of upstate New York known as the "burned-over" district. Fiery preachers from a seemingly endless number of Christian sects had turned the region into a hot-bed of religious debate. People were frantically seeking clear, consistent answers to probing questions about the nature and meaning of Christianity.

At the same time, change was in the air. The new nation was possessed of vast resources and seemingly endless opportunity in the unknown wilderness to the west. Hope combined with a pulsating anxiety about the destiny of the nation and the part that individual settlers were to play in the developing cultural drama. People were literally starved for a new vision; the possibilities were optimal for the emergence of a new religious movement. As we shall see, Joseph Smith's divine revelation that exploded into the Mormon religion not only answered every doctrinal query that smoldered in the hearts of Christian seekers in upstate New York but, at the same time, defined a divine mandate for the settling of the West.

In each case, we will find the prophets of our sectarian religions seizing the moment; call it genius or call it luck, they were able to adroitly play the cards dealt them from the deck of possibility. Mary Baker Eddy's demand that Christian Scientists rely on spiritual healing rather than seeking medical remedies for physical woes would not have been so readily embraced had nineteenth-century doctors known the secrets of penicillin. The Pentecostal revivals of Azusa Street in Los Angeles rumbled into a national movement just days after the great San Francisco earthquake of 1906 seemed to portend that the "end was nigh." In the world of our sectarian religion, even geological possibilities could be used to expand and promote the "new order of things."

Place

Our last category will, of course, be at the heart of our investigation of made-in-America sectarian religions. Place is none other than the state of California. As mentioned, though each religion originated in another part of the country, all found a home in the Golden State. In each case, as we move through our investigation, we will discover unique stories about the relationship of sectarian religions to the California social environment. But, in general, a number of factors contributed to the usually successful implantation of American religions in a California that, in many ways, embodied all the utopian aspirations of a westward moving populace.

One reason that sectarian religions fared well in California is that western-moving settlers tended to toss aside the more restrictive trappings of tradition as they crossed the Continental Divide and entered the open spaces of the West. It was as though the physical openness brought new ideas and new ways of going about the business of living. Californians have always had a penchant for experimenting with cultural styles, and religious innovation was more acceptable than it might have been in the tradition-minded East. There simply was more room to do things, thus people felt less constrained to conform to some imagined norm of religious behavior. For example, though Christian Science emerged in the stodgy corridors of Boston society, today, there are more Christian Scientists in California than in any other state.

Another reason for the success of sectarian religions might be called the "seeker spirit." Settlers who moved west were the kind of people who were naturally dissatisfied with the "old order of things." They endured the dangerous and sometimes disastrous trek to California because just over the next mountain, or just across the raging river lay the culmination of their dreams. Health oriented religions such as Christian Science, New Thought, and Seventh-Day Adventists, found the climate sufficiently supportive of their quest for physical perfection. Mormon missionaries found open ears and open minds in the free spirits who worked the mines and built the railroads. The very excitement of California life added to the Pentecostal fervor as tongues of fire poured down on expectant believers. All in all, California was a place where there were plenty of seekers more than ready to believe in something new.

A third reason for the rise in made-in-America religions at first seems almost paradoxical. Though most Californians express sincere religious leanings, they tended to be "religious" outside of any identifiable religious organization. Sociologists point out that the majority of Americans tend to be "unchurched," that is, they do not belong to a specific church, temple, mosque, etc. Not only does this mean that, in the Golden State, there are usually a lot of people with deeply felt religious feelings who might easily adopt a new religious perspective; it also implies that there are a good number of non-believers or secularists. These would be folks who share the "perfections in paradise" aspirations of sectarian religionists but who seek to accomplish their goals through political rather than religious means.

This phenomenon actually contributed to an "open-market" climate that ultimately was conducive to the spread of sectarian religions. The secular majority acted as a controlling force keeping traditional religious perspectives or any single worldview from commandeering the avenues of power in Californian society. Thus, believers found less prejudice, less antagonism towards their religion and more freedom to practice without constraint. Religious freedom became just a little more free in the pluralistic environment of late nineteenth-century California. Pluralism—a term that denotes the reasonably peaceful co-existence of a variety of worldviews in the same community—simply kept everyone a little more honest in their respective quests to realize a "new order of things."

Of course place, as California, could never have emerged

unless place, as the United States, provided a healthy environment for prophets, promises, plans, and possibilities. In chapter two, we will broaden our vision and concentrate on the social environment of nineteenth- and early twentieth-century America, out of which our sectarian religions emerged.

SOURCES AND FURTHER READING
McGuire, Meredith. *Religion: The Social Context*. Belmont, CA: Wadsworth Press, 1981.
Stark, Rodney, and Bainbridge, William. *The Future of Religion*. Berkeley, CA: University of California Press, 1985.

2 The Chosen and the 'Choosers' in the Land of the Free

In the average history or civics class, it is taught that, in the United States, there is no "established religion." In other words, citizens of this nation are not forced to pay taxes to support a particular religious organization. In addition, the First Amendment to the United States Constitution guarantees that all peoples are free to practice the religion of their choice—or to believe in no religious ideal at all. Thus, as the saying goes, we have, in this country, a "wall separating church and state." Governing bodies at the local, state, and national levels have no business being involved in the "business" of religion.

Legally, of course, separation of church and state *is* a reality in the United States. But at a much more subtle level, as we shall see, religious precepts permeated the social fabric of our culture to such an extent that the United States, at least in the nineteenth and early twentieth centuries, could justifiably be called a "Judeo-Christian" nation. *Myths* drawn from Judaism and Christianity provided a "culture core," which, though never overtly expressed, affected every aspect of the new nation's growth and evolution from the highest levels of policy-making to the most basic social customs that defined life on "Main Street." And, for our purposes, these same myths created just the right religious environment for the emergence of our sectarian new religious movements.

Before we examine the American culture-core and judge its effect on the sectarian impulse, it is important that we sort out the real power and meaning of myths. If the proverbial person-on-the-street is asked to define "myth," the likely answer will be: a false story. And, to be sure, that is how the word is used in our society by anyone from politicians to sportscasters to history teachers. But in the academic study of religion, the term has the opposite—and correct—meaning. *Myths* are the most profoundly *true stories* that can be told.

Of course, when we speak of "truth" regarding myths, we need to understand truth as something different from scientifically verifiable information. Myths are true to believers at a level that is much more experiential, emotional, psychological, even intuitive. A believer does not just *know* a myth; the believer *lives, embodies,* the myth. Above all, the "truth" of myths are found in the powerful ways they affect the *behavior* of believers. Myths are stories that offer human beings paradigms or models for successfully engaging the adventure of life. These sometimes imaginative, sometimes fantastic accounts of super-human strength, endurance, guile, hope, have a number of important functions: they (a) offer ways of ordering experience; (b) inform human beings about themselves and their place in the natural and cultural environments; (c) provide patterns for human behavior; (d) offer explanations for death, pain, change, and suffering as well as avenues for liberation from life's trials and tribulations; (e) provide human beings with meaning, purpose, a sense of reverence for the past and hope for the future.

To illustrate the functions of myth in a familiar setting, we need only consider a family gathering such as Thanksgiving. True, families are not as extended or as tight as they once were in this culture (the loss of agreed upon myths has much to do with this), but the importance of story telling has not lessened even in the most secular of families. Along with the ritual of munching down the turkey and the mashed potatoes, the family experiences a sense of unity and belonging through storytelling. Key family experiences are remembered; perhaps an enjoyable vacation, a tragic event, a humorous action that seems to represent a family member's quirky personality. At each gathering, the family looks forward to telling these stories, and though everyone has heard them a thousand times, they are never boring. They serve the purpose of establishing boundaries about who the family is, what they have done together, where they are headed as a unit. This, on a very small scale, gives you some sense of the power of storytelling as it defines community.

Now imagine how much more powerful these stories might be when they take on mythic proportions. In the case of the United States, scholars who study the religious elements in American culture have identified a mythic base sometimes referred to as *civil religion*. If myths disclose the ultimate reality to human beings, then civil religion in America might best be described as an attempt on the part of American citizens to understand their nation's history and destiny in terms of the great biblical stories. In particular, it has been noted that the United States is an "Old Testament" nation. One reason modern-day Israel and the United States are such good friends goes beyond politics; Israeli and United States citizens share similar mythic precepts about the founding and destiny of their respective nations—a chosen people with a special covenantal relationship with God who protects and guides the nation as long as His people maintain the high ethical demands of that covenant. By covenant, we mean a give-and-take agreement, usually between groups, persons, and/or transcendent beings of unequal power. A simple verbal model for this agreement might go something like "if you do this for me, I'll take care of that for you."

The mythic drama found in the Jewish holy scriptures, the *Torah*, or first five books of the Bible, tells of the making of a people with a special destiny to live freely under moral law. On these "chosen people" is bestowed a "land of milk and honey" where they might grow and prosper—*if* they maintain the high moral standards that God demands of them. To lapse into "immorality" is to break the covenant and, potentially, to lose everything.

If the theory that ancient Israel provides an historical/behavioral model for the United States seems a bit overwrought, consider Jerry Falwell and the rise of the Moral Majority during the Reagan years of the presidency. Ronald Reagan may go down in history as many things; but one role he played to the hilt was that of "High Priest of American Civil Religion." No recent president has been better able to play the harp-strings of the nation's civil religious sentiment than former President Reagan.

Jerry Falwell touched the same chord from the religious perspective. His first book, *Listen America*, reads like a prophetic condemnation of the nation. In essence—and he is writing in 1979, when the festering wounds of the Vietnam War had just been reinfected with the Iranian hostage crisis—he theorizes that America lost its first war and is in economic and cultural demise because American citizens have broken their moral covenant with God. The women's rights movement (which, according to Falwell, was breaking up the family), homosexuality, drugs, pornography and so on, represented moral failures that incurred God's wrath. Unless moral people came out of the closet and renewed their side of the covenant, America would be cut off from the hand of God and perish as a nation. This biblical evaluation of America's crisis was so intensely received by a large number of American people that, by 1988, a Pentecostal minister, Pat Robertson, actually got close to the Republican nomination for president.

Understandably, if these mythic elements could be taken so seriously in the modern, technologically oriented, secular world of the late twentieth century, they held enormous power in the previous century. And, when you mix in important elements of the Christian mythos, the tension between morality and prosperity, hope and failure becomes even more intense. For instance, the Christian teaching of the Second Coming of Jesus was interpreted in two somewhat paradoxical ways. One version of the mythic drama called for the creation of the "kingdom of heaven on earth" as preparation for Jesus' return. In this scenario, American believers were called upon to build a perfect world which would be suitable for the thousand year reign of Jesus that would follow His return.

The other scenario saw the world as an essentially doomed place; the faithful remnant had been brought to the "wilderness" of a new continent to await the final apocalyptic battle between the forces of good and the minions of Satan. Of course, one sign that indicated salvation for a believer was a productive, prosperous life. So though the beliefs about the meaning, nature, and destiny of the nation might differ, the *behavior* of the believers, in response to the challenge of cultural change, was practically identical—be industrious, maintain high moral standards, wait and watch for the Lord.

In fact, during inevitable times of major cultural change as the nation grew and prospered, these mythic elements from ancient biblical stories guided national policy and grounded the nation in Judeo-Christian ideals. In the nineteenth century, American citizens lived out the successes and failures of the nation according to these mythic precepts. In particular, *religious revivals*, evangelism, witnessing to the Lord, getting saved, getting back into that covenantal bond with God, became a powerful force for cleansing society—especially during times of high anxiety characteristic of social change.

Actually, we can identify two distinct "streams" of revivalism—which bring us directly to our sectarian religions. One stream, the establishment stream, flowed into and out of Protestant Christianity. The other stream gushed forth from the same pool of social needs and desires but forged sectarian rivulets—our made-in-America religions. Countries are very much like people when it comes to experiencing challenges. Fear of the unknown creates tension which, in turn, pushes people, individually or collectively, toward a reexamination of the familiar and preparation for difficulties involved in making the leap from old to new.

For instance, a common experience for many Americans is the major move to a distant town or city. The potent mixture of anxiety and excitement that surrounds such a move forces family members to rally around a set of values, customs, and talents that are unique to the family. This is natural since it is necessary to work together in order to meet and overcome the difficulties such a move creates. At the same time, in adapting to the new circumstances, the family changes and, though the memories of the past are still cherished, it soon becomes evident that the "old ways" of going about life will no longer work in the new environment.

Similarly, in the history of the United States, when the country was forced by a variety of circumstances—political, social, environmental, etc.—to "make a move," the aforementioned set of values we have called the *culture core* underwent a reevaluation and a retooling so that the nation could adapt to new cultural circumstances. Since the elements of the culture core were inherently religious, these periods of change, sometimes lasting thirty or forty years, had a profound impact on the way people went about the business of life on a day-to-day basis. Out of the energetic religious revivals that characterized these periods, Protestant Christian groups redefined the nature of God, human destiny, and the meaning of Christianity, but retained enough of the essential elements of Protestantism to remain within the denominational boundaries of, say, Methodism, Lutheranism, Presbyterianism, or Baptist groups.

Our sectarian religions, on the other hand, simply pushed the boundaries a bit further until, like beads of mercury separating from a larger pool, something new, something different was created.

It was from two of these periods of major cultural change that our sectarian religions emerge; one following the American Revolution and extending into the first decades of the nineteenth century; the other following the traumatic upheaval of the Civil War and extending into the first years of the twentieth century. In each case, American citizens were forced to question the elements of the culture core: what did it mean to be chosen people; once chosen, how was the nation to go about pursuing its destiny? What were the moral demands that would insure divine blessings? And always, if that destiny became elusive, the smoldering embers of religious zeal could be stoked to insure that the covenantal fire would never burn out. These were exciting times, times for new visions, times when the "chosen people" were called upon to reach down deep within themselves in order to make choices; choices, they hoped, that would guide the nation past the wave-splashed rocks of cultural upheaval and into the still harbor of renewed security and prosperity.

Cultural Challenge in the Early Nineteenth Century: The Birth of Mormonism, Adventism, and Spiritualism

Freedom and plenty are a wonderful combination but, like the lottery-player who wins a million dollars, right choices determine whether the windfall is a blessing or a curse. The early decades of the nineteenth century were filled with endless possibilities. The nation was, in fact, free from colonial constraints; beyond the coastal settlements, a land of immense wealth and opportunity stretched as far as the eye or the imagination could see. Truly, the people of this new nation must have felt that God was "on their side" since everywhere they turned they seemed to be beneficiaries of divine providence.

But all this good fortune was not without responsibilities; and, as is often the case, impending responsibilities create anxiety. How were the "chosen people" supposed to go about settling the wilderness? How were those all-important elements of the culture core to be lived out? In response to this crisis of opportunity, Protestant Christian leaders called for revivalism and reform which soon took the nation by storm. From the stodgy seminaries in Boston to the great "camp meetings" out along the frontier trails, a great wave of religious enthusiasm swept across the country, out of which a set of ideals emerged that redefined the meaning and destiny of the fledgling United States. At the heart of these ideals was the deeply held belief that, like the ancient Israelites, God had given His people a land so that, for the glory of God, a people would grow and prosper and be a "light for all the nations." It was, therefore, up to the people to be about the business of building this great nation. The combination of religious zeal with unlimited natural resources turned the nation into an energetic pack of doers and joiners. A "can-do" spirit energized most Protestant groups as they vigorously went about the business of moral reform, evangelism, and the creation of innumerable missions, associations, and societies designed to gird up Americans for the grand trek toward destiny.

As mentioned, religious ideals emerged from the Protestant experience which, in the possession of the religiously imaginative, became the spark that ignited our new religious movements. One expert on American religious history, Sydney E. Ahlstrom, identifies these as (a) perfectionism, (b) millennialism, (c) universalism, and (d) illuminism. As we explore each of these ideals, remember that the four elements worked as a combined catalyst in the minds and souls of nineteenth-century believers giving them the freedom to embark on journeys into unexplored spiritual territory.

The Protestant settlers who arrived on this continent in the 1600s brought with them a confining set of theological concepts. Two of the most stultifying were "original sin" and "predestination." Put simply, these doctrines convinced believers that they were incorrigible "sinners," doomed by the curse upon Adam and Eve to live a life of moral failure and, on Judgment Day, stand before an angry God. "Predestination" implied that there was really nothing a person could do about his or her fate. God already had predestined that some would be saved and some would be damned to hell.

The story is a long and fascinating one—well beyond the scope of this chapter—but, over time, this taut theological rope could no longer tie down the religious imagination of freedom-seeking colonists. As this unraveling process entered the nineteenth century, there was a sense that the hand of God had delivered the people into this "promised land" for a special destiny—to build the

"Kingdom of God" on the North American continent. Thus, spiritual and social *perfection* became, not something to be attained in some distant heavenly existence, but a real possibility here, on earth. Within the Protestant churches, perfectionism found its religious expression in movements such as the Holiness groups that emerged from within the Methodist Church. Within our early sectarian religions, we can identify elements of perfectionism in the Mormon quest to build a sacred community and the zealous way Adventists and later Jehovah's Witnesses prepared themselves for imminent salvation. Of course, perfectionism is most obvious in later nineteenth-century religions such as Christian Science and New Thought which we will touch on momentarily.

If people were now capable of attaining spiritual perfection, there had to be a reason for it. In the minds of both Mormon and Adventist believers, the reason had to be that the end was near. Millennialism, the belief that the current corrupt age would end with the beginning of Christ's triumphal thousand-year reign, was a highly potent religious motivator during the early decades of the nineteenth century. As we shall see in the respective chapters on Mormonism and Adventism, Mormons and Adventists saw themselves as "latter-day saints" called to restore the true Christian community and build Zion on the North American continent.

Adventism grew out of the millennial fervor surrounding the preaching of one William Miller, who, after making some calculations based on the biblical book of Daniel, predicted that the second coming of Jesus would occur in the year 1843. As we mentioned in chapter one, the Pentecostal movement was given a charge of spiritual energy when leaders identified the San Francisco earthquake of 1906 as a sign that the end was near. Though these will be our most obvious examples of millennialism, each of our sectarian religions, to some degree, embraced the millennial idea that a new age of spiritual possibility was about to dawn.

Universalism and Illuminism round out nineteenth-century religious ideals. Universalism was a direct denial of the older theological notion of predestination. The "can-do" spirit of the early nineteenth-century revivals suggested that all people could be saved; it was only a matter of identifying, then following the most direct path to salvation. Certainly, in this "new order of things" that was the United States, new paths would open up. Illuminism was the belief that new light, new revelations, would pour down upon the chosen people, igniting new religious movements. The combination of these two ideals, as they took root in the minds of sectarian religious leaders, gave a green light to religious innovation. Spiritualism played on both these themes in the sense that death did not separate us from loved ones and that human beings still "shuffling around this mortal coil" could, in fact, gain wisdom from more spiritually evolved beings in the higher realms.

However, the best example of the universalism/illuminism combination can be found in the Mormon story. The divine revelation received by Joseph Smith contained a number of teachings that "corrected" mistakes in standard Christian doctrine. One of these inaccuracies concerned original sin and damnation. According to the Mormon perspective, people were not cursed with sin because Adam and Eve decided to fool around in the Garden of Eden; people brought sin upon themselves and, concurrently, had the personal power to cease their sinful ways. Thus, universal salvation was a real possibility in the Mormon worldview. Illuminism as continued revelation also characterizes Mormonism. Even after the *Book of Mormon* was revealed to Joseph Smith, God continued to speak to the prophet and, after his death, to his successors. In fact, to this day, Mormons rely on new revelations, new light, whenever a crisis threatens or a theological point needs to be clarified.

Cultural Challenge in the Late Nineteenth Century: The Birth of Christian Science, New Thought, the Jehovah's Witnesses, and Pentecostalism

Obviously, the Civil War had an impact on American culture like a mega-earthquake along the San Andreas fault. In particular, President Abraham Lincoln defined this national tragedy in decidedly Old Testament terms. Following the biblical model of sin, punishment, and redemption, Lincoln saw the conflict as divine punishment for the sin of slavery. Like ancient Israel, the promised land was torn asunder; only the bloody sacrifices of battle assuaged the anger of God and saved the divine experiment that was the United States. Now in this terrible time of grief and repentance the churches were called upon to provide new visions, new choices for the chosen people.

But what were those choices to be? Having just come out of a soul-shaking war, the culture core of the nation was scrambled into two equally tempestuous revolutions: an intellectual revolution coupled with enormous socioeconomic change. New ways of perceiving the world present in the intellectual revolution threatened American civil religion on two fronts. First, the thinking, writings, and scholarly investigations of Charles Darwin, Sigmund Freud, and Karl Marx completely undermined the covenantal biblical notions of a transcendent God who could choose a people for a special destiny. Darwin's theory of evolution seemed to suggest that human beings were not made in the image of a moral God but had, in fact, evolved rather randomly over billions of years. So much for the Genesis account. Freud's psychoanalytic theories undercut the early nineteenth-century "can-do" spirit. How could people possibly save themselves if they were not even in control of their own thoughts and emotions? And Marx dropped another bomb on the ideal of a God-driven national quest: God did not determine historical events; the cold, hard economic realities of haves against have-nots moved history down an inescapable path toward revolution. In other words, the "chosen people" really had no choice at all! Their collective fate was determined, not by some exalted spiritual force, but by material forces, over which they had no control.

As if this was not enough, the Bible itself seemed to come under attack from scholars who, for the first time, were examining the book, not as a sacred text, but as a literary-historical account that could be examined from an objective, critical standpoint. Was the Bible "God-breathed" inerrant scripture? Or was it the work of human beings whose perceptions were just as culturally-bound and potentially inaccurate as any account of human history? For many, this Higher Biblical Criticism, as it was called, undermined the authority of the Bible and, thus, called into question every element in America's Bible-based culture core.

At the same time the intellectual, theological, and cultural underpinnings of the nation came under attack, society was undergoing massive changes in the late nineteenth century. Industrialization, immigration, and urbanization combined to push American society into a complex sociocultural labyrinth without a map for guidance or leaders who possessed the intuitive qualities necessary for successful travel through the maze. The simplicity of agrarian/small-town values—voluntary cooperation, rugged individualism tempered by community spirit, implicitly accepted

Protestant moral precepts such as thrift, sobriety, modesty, hard work, honesty—seemed to set one at a disadvantage in the exploding urban jungles characterized by slums, crime, labor unrest, political corruption, capitalist exploitation, etc. Furthermore, the immigration of non-Anglo-Saxon, non-English-speaking, non-Protestant peoples into a once homogeneous society caused a severe national identity crisis. People were in genuine distress as to the nature and meaning of their own lives, not to mention the life of the nation.

As we shall see in our respective discussions of Christian Science, New Thought, the Jehovah's Witnesses, and Pentecostalism, these perilous times cried out for new choices to be made in "the land of the free." Calling on the same religious ideals—perfectionism, millennialism, universalism, and illuminism—the charismatic leaders of these made-in-America religions shared a destiny in that they would redefine what it meant to be religious in a much more complex world. Now let us turn to our first sectarian religion—Mormonism. In the following chapters, using our prophet, promise, plan, and possibility model, we will examine the religious motivation that spawned this great worldview, meet the leaders, chronicle the organizational development, and, most importantly, explore the impact of Mormon believers on the place that is California.

SOURCES AND FURTHER READING

Ahlstrom, Sydney E. *A Religious History of the American People*. Garden City, NY: Doubleday and Co., 1975. 2 Vols.
McLoughlin, William G. *Revivals, Awakenings, and Reform*. Chicago: University of Chicago Press, 1978.

3 The Mormons in California: Then and Now

The story of the Mormons, more properly referred to as the Church of Jesus Christ of Latter-Day Saints, may well be the most stirring and fascinating story in American religious history. And, like all good stories that capture the imagination, it is a tale of struggle, persecution, perseverance, and enormous achievement bringing about vindication and rewards to the larger-than-life characters who people the narrative. To be sure, the Mormon story is a success story. Today, as other nineteenth-century religions such as Christian Science and many of the varied New Thoughts groups seem to be headed toward the institutional graveyard, Mormonism is being touted by religious historians as the next great world religion. Since 1970, the church has more than doubled its substantial membership and is quickly spreading around the globe!

If one were to attempt to write a book entitled "How to Start a Successful Religion," there could be no better model to follow than that provided by Mormonism. As we will see in this chapter, Joseph Smith, our prophet, had the vision and tenacity to capture the spiritual energy of early American citizens and with it, generate a "new order of things" that, in many ways, was an exact expression of the most sacred ideals on which the country was founded. The only way to explain the survival of the religion which, from its infancy, engendered massive persecution on the part of non-Mormons, is to recognize this nearly perfect match between religious ideal and political reality. And, in terms of church leadership, Joseph Smith's descendants, beginning with the famous Utah-bound Brigham Young, were able to nurture and expand on the prophet's vision.

The California chapter in this grand Mormon saga is as powerful as it is ironic. Energized by their remarkable zeal to gather the faithful to Zion and spread the gospel, Mormons were some of the first Americans to settle in the state during and following the Mexican War (1846), when the beautiful and bountiful territory was wrested from the hands of Mexico. As we will see, under the leadership of a classic American pioneer in Mormon garb, Samuel Brannan, Mormons traveled by ship to California, landing, in 1846, in the sleepy port of Yerba Buena. He and his fellow travelers were among the first Americans to assist in the transformation process which would turn Yerba Buena into a rather well-known city by the name of San Francisco.

To the south, a Mormon battalion, sent by Brigham Young to liberate California from the Mexicans in 1847, comprised the first Americans to raise the flag over Los Angeles. As early as 1851, Mormon settlements sprouted in San Bernardino.

And yet there is an element of irony surrounding the California story. Almost from the beginning, for all the possibility that California represented for the creation of Zion on the North American continent, tension developed between the Mormon community in Utah and the much less populous and less powerful community in California. In some ways, the attempts by the Utah church to cling to the reigns of power stifled the early growth of the California community. Today, however, it is California Mormons who may well be providing the model for the globalization of this hugely successful worldview.

But we are getting ahead of ourselves. This epic drama begins, as most do, in very humble surroundings, in this case, the life and times of one Joseph Smith, an imaginative, often perplexing, searching young man who would become prophet of the "new order of things" that became Mormonism.

The early years in Joseph Smith's life were, indeed, humble. Vermont-born in 1805 to a poor farming family, he moved, in 1815 at the age of 10, to western New York where his father continued to struggle against the exigencies of agricultural life. By his teenage years, young Joseph had discovered that his interests lay somewhere beyond the horse and plow. Like many a young seeker, he became entranced with the religious fervor of the time, testing any number of teachings for the "truth" about God and the meaning of life.

On a warm spring day in 1820, an event occurred that would forever change Joseph's life—not to mention American religious history. Tormented by the conflicting doctrinal statements proclaimed by the myriad revivalist preachers who "burned over" this district of western New York, our soon-to-be prophet retired to the woods to seek solace in prayer. What followed was an encounter with the divine which, in his own words, he described as follows:

My object in going to inquire of the Lord was to know which of all the sects was right, that I might know which to join. No sooner, therefore, did I get possession of myself, so as to be able to speak, then I asked the personages who stood above me in the light, which of all the sects was right—and which I should join. I was answered that I must join none of them, for they were all wrong, and the personage who addressed me said that all their creeds were an abomination in His sight: that those professors were all corrupt; that 'they draw near to me with their lips, but their hearts are far from me; they teach for doctrines the commandments of me: having a form of godliness, but they deny the power thereof.' He again forbade me to join with any of them: and many other things did he say unto me, which I cannot write at this time. When I came to myself again, I found myself lying on my back, looking up into heaven. When the light had departed, I had no strength; but soon recovering in some degree, I went home. (Joseph Smith, *History of the Church.* Salt Lake City: Deseret Book Company, 1902-1912.)

From our perspective, Joseph Smith's prophetic call was nothing less than a divine decree to start a "new order of things." If none of the churches possessed the right doctrine, it was up to Joseph to do what Jesus, from a Christian viewpoint, had done for Judaism—to bring to light a new Testament and, thus, realign humanity with the divine will.

Shortly after his first numinous experience, another celestial visitor, the angel Moroni, directed Joseph to the Hill Cumorah where, many centuries before, gold plates containing the *Book of Mormon* were buried. When the hieroglyphics were translated by Joseph using two divining stones (Urim and Thumim), a fascinating, if rambling, 500-page historical account emerged that not only linked the young American nation with the biblical past but gave its inhabitants the possibility of playing the leading role in the "latter" days of God's great historical drama. For Joseph Smith's revelation called for nothing less than gathering "the Saints" and building Zion— God's kingdom on Earth on the very land that "mom and pop pioneer" were struggling to tame. With the *Book of Mormon* in hand, Joseph Smith offered his flock not only a promise, that "the Saints" (as in Latter-Day Saints), with God's blessing, would restore the true Christian church on the North American continent, but also a plan; a model that revealed how that enormously important task would be accomplished.

The *Book of Mormon* relates a sacred history of the pre-Columbian inhabitants of North America. Echoing the "lost tribes of Israel" theme, descendants of Joseph (the biblical Joseph as opposed to our prophet) came to this continent in the year 600 B.C. only to fall into tribal conflict between the "good" Nephites and the "wicked" Lamanites. Racism aside (the Nephites were white-skinned while the Laminites were dark), the descendants of the Lamanites were said to be the American Indians which, to the mind of the early nineteenth-century citizen, seemed a plausible explanation for their often antagonistic presence on the local scene.

In any event, the Lamanites prevailed, until, by the year 384 C.E., only Mormon and his son Moroni were left. God directed Moroni to bury the gold plates containing this sacred history until the time when the Nephites' descendants were spiritually ready to establish Zion, the New Jerusalem, in the "latter days." As we mentioned in the first chapter, in a single stroke of religious genius, Joseph Smith injected the aforementioned culture core of the infant nation with a divine elixir. A young, searching nation with an inferiority complex, seemingly relegated to the backyard of civilization, suddenly was at the very heart of a divine plan that began 3,900 years ago with Abraham's call. At last, with the *Book of Mormon* in hand, all personal and collective spiritual confusion was assuaged. Joseph Smith, the prophet, revealed a new order of things that was equal to the energy of a new nation with seemingly unlimited natural resources and untapped potential.

As is the case with most of the original prophets of America's sectarian religions, Joseph Smith never ventured to California. The full scope of early Mormon development is, obviously, beyond the means of this short account. But from the very beginning of Mormonism as an established religion, persecution hounded "the Saints," even as their numbers increased dramatically. It is difficult to determine whether religious prejudice was the spark that caused non-Mormons to attack members of this "new order of things." Certainly, if religion amounted to anything in the souls of the American pioneers, it expressed itself in the form of "Bible-believin' evangelical revivalist Protestantism." And Mormonism represented a serious threat to the authority of standard Christian teachings.

More likely, the cause of enmity toward Mormons was a much more mundane, and common, human failing: simple jealousy. If the plan was to build Zion, the promise unfolded as an ongoing set of revelations that came to Joseph Smith; a set of doctrines that shaped a new breed of believers who were primed to overcome adversity and achieve success. And physically, psychologically, and spiritually, nineteenth-century America provided both possibility and the place for the realization of that success.

At the heart of Smith's teachings is a perspective on reality that might best be described as materialistic perfectionism. The pursuit of material success and the drive toward worldly progress were overwhelmingly powerful values in nineteenth-century American culture. What Smith did was to imbue these key motivating forces with transcendent potency. Mormonism teaches that matter, the material universe, is sacred, the very substance of divinity. Human suffering is not the result of punishment for "original sin," but represents the failure of human beings to know and live by the laws and ordinances of God. God is not conceived of as an infinite creator who controls all aspects of human existence. The world has always existed; God is a finite being, similar in substance to the human spirit or soul, only more evolved. Good comes to human beings, not by relying on or petitioning a distant God for assistance, but through effort and accomplishment which, inevitably, lead to appropriate rewards. In fact, all Mormons may one day rise to the spiritual realm where, in some celestial heaven, they can become "gods."

The above description of Mormon doctrines is, in no way, meant to be a comprehensive listing of Joseph Smith's promise. What we are trying to grasp is the spiritual force that generated that remarkable Mormon zeal and the accompanying capacity to overcome all obstacles and create, build, expand with seemingly super-human effort. Using our terminology, when a promise and a plan arise in a place, a culture that embraces values that, in turn, create a social atmosphere perfectly suited to the realization of that plan, the possibilites are endless. In fact, everywhere Mormons settled, from New York to Kirkland, Ohio, to Missouri, to Nauvoo, Illinois, then on to Utah, they out-farmed, out-built, out-banked, out-reproduced, and outraged their non-Mormon neighbors. In addition, they toyed with a very explosive combination; they were, at once, an exclusivist religious group that, nevertheless, felt called upon to proselytize non-believers. This combination of "we have it and you don't" mixed with obvious success and a certain proclivity on the part of early Americans to settle things with a gun, brought all manner of horror down upon "the Saints."

Joseph Smith became the victim of this type of horror in Carthage, Illinois on June 27, 1844. Controversy rages to this day concerning the details of the prophet's death, but no one argues with the fact that a mob pumped a fatal number of musket rounds into the body of a true American original. Little did they know that this violent act would simply fuel new Mormon zeal and send "the Saints" off to even greater deeds; deeds that included the crossing of the Sierra Nevada into California.

A single incident captures the spirit of the Mormon experience in California. As mentioned, the intrepid Mormon leader, Samuel Brannan, sailed "around the horn" on the good ship *Brooklyn* from New York harbor, and landed with a band of Mormon colonists in the town that was to become San Francisco. The year was 1846, a pivotal time in the early years of Mormon development.

The prophet was two years dead. Brigham Young and "the Saints" were suffering out on the Mormon trail, somewhere between the tragedy that was Nauvoo and the hope of a safe and fertile valley, far beyond "gentile" (a Mormon term for non-Mormons) persecution, where, finally, Zion could be established. The miraculous entry into the Salt Lake valley had yet to occur.

If we could "walk for a mile" in Samuel Brannan's moccasins, we would look out on a California that few can imagine today. A real paradise, a land of temperate clime, natural harbors, abundant resources, and seemingly endless open space where an industrious, God-inspired people could do nothing less than prosper. Understandably, Brannan was convinced that he had found the place where Zion would be founded, and, after lending a hand in the civilizing of Yerba Buena, set out to find a spot where Brigham Young and the main body of the Church would eventually settle.

Assured that it was only a matter of time before the westward-bound Mormons crossed the Sierra Nevada, Brannan and the California colonists prepared a "gathering place" at the juncture of the San Joaquin and Stanislaus rivers in the San Joaquin Valley, a place they called "New Hope." Time passed, however, and no Mormon wagon train appeared on the horizon.

Not a man given to waiting around, Brannan decided to head eastward with hopes of meeting up with Young and sharing the good news that was California. After crossing the deserts and mountainous regions that we now know as Nevada and Utah, he finally met up with the vanguard of the party and actually accompanied Brigham Young on the historic entry into the Salt Lake valley.

Although the meeting between Brannan and Young, the incident referred to at the beginning of this section, was frustrating for Brannan, it was, in a way, prophetic. No amount of persuasion, cajoling, even threatening could convince Young to continue westward into California. Zion was to be founded in Utah. California, at best, could only be an outlying settlement, a satellite orbiting around the center of the Mormon world. The seeds of tension were planted between Utah and California Mormons. Disappointed and humiliated, Brannan headed back across the Sierras to serve the small, but growing Mormon community in California.

If it is difficult to understand why Brigham Young ignored Brannan's exhortations to build Zion in the Golden State, or worse, if it seems like a colossal blunder on the part of this otherwise great Mormon leader, we must, again, try to visualize the situation from Young's perspective. First, the Mormons endured unspeakable horrors during their expulsion from Illinois and painful sojourn on the Mormon trail. Death, disease, starvation, armed conflict with Native Americans and non-Mormons all plagued the Saints on their journey westward. It is simply possible that, as their leader, Young knew that his people had reached the limit of human endurance.

Second, Brannan's account of a California paradise may not have struck "Garden of Eden" chords from Young's perspective. Due to the years of persecution, the goal of the arduous Mormon trek was to find "a place apart"; a gathering place far from seemingly inevitable animosity of non-Mormons who were either unable of or unwilling to accept the "truth" of this new revelation. Fertile fields, beautiful harbors, navigable rivers, precious minerals like gold sounded wonderful but would also attract non-Mormons in droves. Thus, the empty, arid land of the Salt Lake valley offered sanctuary that California probably could not sustain.

Third, an intriguing question arises as to the Mormon political self-image in 1846-47. "To be or not to be" American posed a real dilemma for the Mormon leadership as well as the rank-and-file believer. As we have already seen, Joseph Smith's revelation imbued the American culture core with new spiritual purpose. At the same time, it was a non-believing majority of Americans who branded Mormons as traitors and heretics. In fact, Joseph Smith's declaration of candidacy for the presidency of the United States was an important factor in bringing down the ire of the non-Mormon citizenry of Illinois.

California had just been won from Mexico and was clearly designated as American territory, not unlike Utah, but the focus of the war brought immediate attention to the potential this territory offered for American citizens. Perhaps Young, justifiably, saw more political complications and less opportunity to create a separate nation in California and, despite Brannan's glowing report, looked out on the Salt Lake valley and declared, "This is home!"

In any event, during Brannan's return to the California settlement, two strands of our story literally became entwined. As he descended the trail westward from the heights of the Sierra Nevada, Brannan was surprised to come across fellow Mormons; members of the Mormon Battalion who, having done their duty in Southern California, were preparing to brave the dangers of a late fall crossing in order to return to their families in Utah.

The story of the Mormon Battalion provides another testimonial to the zeal of the Saints. Only months after the Mormons fled Nauvoo in 1846, Brigham Young made the decision that, in spite of the crimes perpetrated upon them by the gentiles, he would demonstrate Mormon loyalty to the United States by sending an armed Battalion to assist in the fight against Mexico. In August of 1846, the troops, under command of a Colonel P. St. George Cooke, left Fort Leavenworth, Kansas and embarked on what was described as the longest infantry march in recorded history.

Literally carving out the Santa Fe trail, the Battalion finally arrived at Warner's Ranch on January 21, 1847—worn, weary, half-starved, and unfortunately, too late to share in the decisive battles that tore California from Mexico's grasp. After recuperating in the San Diego area at the deserted Mission San Luis Rey, on March 19, 1847, the main body of the Battalion journeyed up the coast to Los Angeles. Ravaged by war and populated by thieves, drunks, killers, prostitutes, and gamblers (not unlike today), Los Angeles cried out for some kind of stabilizing force. Apparently, the Mormon army provided just that, helping citizens to reclaim their streets, rebuild their houses and businesses, and rid the surrounding area of marauding bandits.

During their stay in Los Angeles, members of the Battalion built Fort Moore and, in their efforts to roust the thieves and raiders who made life miserable for ranchers in the mountainous regions east of the city, scouted out the Cajon Pass and San Bernardino areas. This was important extracurricular activity since, in a few years, Mormon colonists would return to settle in this area.

With the war over and their term of enlistment fulfilled, the men of the Mormon Battalion mustered out of service on July 20, 1847, faced with the choice of staying on in Los Angeles or returning to their families in Utah. All but the unattached chose to purchase horses and wagons and head northward toward the Sacramento valley as a first step toward the final eastward plunge homeward. But a change in itinerary was in store for them due to the chance encounter with Samuel Brannan.

Perhaps because the Battalion veterans had seen the Golden State, Brannan was much more successful in convincing them to stay in California than he had been in persuading Brigham Young that Zion lay on the westward side of the Sierra. Again, underscoring the subtle tension that seemed to develop from the very beginning between Utah and California Mormons, Brannan told the ex-soldiers that the situation in Utah seemed hopeless and that, in a year or two, after crops failed and resources petered out, the Saints would realize that California was the true "gathering place" and head out to join the California colony. Surely no subterfuge was involved on the part of Brannan; no doubt, he firmly believed this scenario would be realized.

Most of the Mormons who followed Brannan's advice and stayed in California found work on the American River building a sawmill for one Captain John Sutter. If the name sounds familiar, he was *the* Sutter, the gentleman who purportedly launched the single event that would forever change California: the Gold Rush of 1849. Indeed, Mormons had a direct hand in the discovery of gold and many, such as Samuel Brannan, rode the Gold Rush to fame and prominence in the early California community. In fact, it was Brannan, in one of his many roles as a San Francisco newspaper publisher, who first publicized the discovery of gold to the world.

After a year of frenetic activity in the gold fields, the former Battalion members began to despair of their families and wonder why Brigham Young had not brought the Saints to share in the enormous riches of California. Finally, as all the rest of the world was scrambling toward California in a fit of gold hysteria, these men turned their backs on unlimited wealth and followed the pull of family and religion back to the arid settlement and harsh agricultural life in Utah.

The above events in early California history bring us to yet another strand in the Mormon saga, the establishment of a thriving community in San Bernardino. As early as May 1847, Captain Jefferson Hunt of the Mormon Battalion, who had spent a good deal of time chasing bandits in the San Bernardino mountains, wrote Brigham Young asking for permission to purchase a huge tract of land in the area for a new Mormon settlement. However, when Hunt returned to Utah after his service, he ran into the same Young obstinacy that Brannan had encountered; the church was to remain in Utah and was not to be divided.

Rebuffed but not bowed, Captain Hunt took on the job of guiding a wagon train of non-Mormon gold seekers across the mountains into California by the southern route through Cajon Pass. An historical footnote to this otherwise successful journey finds twenty-seven wagoners, struck with gold fever, leaving the train and striking out due west through the desert. We now call the place of their demise "Death Valley." In any event, once again returning to Utah and ever more enthused about the prospects of a Mormon colony in California, Hunt finally convinced Young to call for volunteers to establish a mission in the Southern California area. Legend has it that Brigham Young called his people together and, expecting perhaps fifty volunteers, was appalled when over five hundred stepped forward to make the trek. Nevertheless, he appointed Amasa Lyman and Charles Rich as special missionaries to head up the project.

The expedition left Salt Lake City in February of 1851 and arrived at a fertile site below Cajon Pass in June of that year. Borrowing funds from their well-heeled brethren to the north who had remained in the gold fields, the settlers purchased a 32,509-acre tract, the Lugo Grant, for the sum of $77,500. Immediately, these industrious colonists set about laying out the townsite that is, today, the city of San Bernardino, as well as planting 1,300 acres of wheat in the surrounding fields.

Again, an element of irony enters our story of the California Mormons. The San Bernardino colony met with enormous success. Crops flourished, schools and churches were built, and, under the direction of Lyman and Rich, San Bernardino not only was the Mormon center in Southern California but a thriving, bustling city threatening Los Angeles in terms of prosperity and promise. In fact, in 1853, Jefferson Hunt was elected to the California State Legislature and, by 1856, the city of San Bernardino, peopled by non-Mormons and Mormons alike, was the hub of trade and culture in the area. If all had gone well, there seems little doubt that Southern California would have superseded the Salt Lake valley as the center of Mormondom. But history was to repeat itself, and the Mormons, once again, found themselves looking down the barrel of a gentile gun.

Of course the usual jealousy-related animosity reared its head on the part of non-Mormons, but it was to be a much larger threat that would ultimately doom the San Bernardino community, at least as far as Mormon presence was concerned. By the fall of 1857, reacting to anti-Mormon sentiment on a national scale, President James Buchanan launched the "Utah Expedition." Salacious rumors of polygamy and sedition going on in the Mormon Zion enraged the general populace, and the Utah Expeditionary Force, under command of Albert Sidney Johnston, was dispatched toward Salt Lake City.

Brigham Young, who was Governor of the Utah territory at the time, expected the worst. After all, beautifully constructed Mormon communities had been burnt to the ground and Mormons slaughtered in each of the previous attempts at establishing Zion. Matters were not helped by a distressing event that had occurred in August of that year, the so-called "Mountain Meadows massacre." Mistaking a civilian wagon train for an advance party of the U.S. Army, Mormon militiamen and their Native American allies wiped out an entire wagon train on the southern Utah trail. The cry for revenge reverberated throughout the gentile world.

As the U.S. Army closed in on Salt Lake City, Brigham Young felt called upon to reunite the Saints from all outlying areas. In November of 1857, instructions were issued to the Mormons in the San Bernardino community to immediately return to Utah with all possible haste in preparation for the assault on Zion. The Saints were forced to sell out to non-Mormons at a loss, and, for all intents and purposes, the last possibility for a California Zion was lost to history.

Certainly, some Mormons returned after the fortunate peaceful settlement of the Utah situation but never again in a colonial sense. California would not be a separate Mormon place, but another American state where Mormons would strike a balance between exclusivity and assimilation. They returned to a "gentile" land and promptly set about settling into a more diverse culture, contributing, and, above all, growing in numbers. From the mid-nineteenth century to the early years of this century, exciting events traded places with quiet, steady growth so that, by the turn of the century, we find a bustling population of around 5,000 Mormons in the Southern California region. Of course that number would quickly double, double again, and continue to grow as the "can-do" spirit of California attracted more of these industrious people. Thus, in a final touch of irony, today we find the California Mormons, once relegated to the backyard of the Mormon kingdom, growing at more than twice the rate of the Utah Mormons.

SOURCES AND FURTHER READINGS

Ahlstrom, Sydney E. *A Religious History of the American People.* Garden City, NY: Doubleday and Co., 1975. 2 vols.

Albanese, Catherine L. *America: Religions and Religion.* Belmont, CA: Wadsworth Publishing Co., 1981.

Bailey, Paul. "The Church of Jesus Christ of Latter-Day Saints" in *The Religious Heritage of Southern California: A Bicentennial Survey,* ed., Francis J. Weber. Los Angeles: Interreligious Council, 1976.

Bishop, Guy M. "'We Are Rather Weaker in Righteousness Than in Numbers'; The Mormon Colony at San Bernardino, California, 1851-1857," in *Religion and Society in the American West,* eds. Carl Guraneri and David Alvarez. Lanham, MD: University Press of America, 1987.

Kotkin, Joel. "Mission from Utah" in *California Magazine.* July, 1991.

Melton, Gordon J. *The Encyclopedia of American Religions,* 3rd Edition. Detroit: Gale Research, 1989.

4 The End of the World Comes to Continent's End: Adventism in California

In America the belief in the imminent Second Coming of Christ to earth is known as Adventism. Whether or not you are familiar with the term, more than likely you have met an Adventist. The Jehovah's Witness who comes to your door once a year and offers you a copy of the *Watchtower* is, for instance, an Adventist. He or she fervently believes that the end of the world as we know it is just around the corner and that a radically new and better one will take its place. Evil will finally be destroyed, you'll be told, and only those who have remained faithful Christians will enjoy everlasting life in an earthly paradise.

The Witnesses, however, while perhaps the most visible Adventist group today, are far from being the only group who await this wondeful transformation. Adventism in many guises has been a long-lasting, widespread, and influential promise in America since the nation's inception. It has also been a promise to which some in California—supposedly itself a paradise on earth—have also found themselves irresistably drawn.

Adventism is in fact but one variety of millennialism, one of the four major themes characteristic of American religion and culture. The goal of this chapter is to locate Adventism in the larger millennial currents of the nation, while at the same time following the career of two specific Adventist groups in the history of California during the late nineteenth and early twentieth centuries. The story

of the early presence of the Seventh-Day Adventists and the Jehovah's Witnesses in the Golden State will tell us a lot about the
changing possibilites for this particular promise in what was then a
rapidly changing place.

Millennialism and Adventism in America

Strictly speaking, millennialism refers to the thousand years of
Christ's reign on earth as foretold in the Book of Revelation at the
end of the New Testament. The myth of the coming millennium has
exerted a powerful influence on the imaginations of people
throughout the history of Christianity—so powerful, in fact, that
centuries after its first articulation it became part of the mythic identity of the United States. However, as we mentioned in chapter two,
the myth of the millennium in the United States has actually been
interpreted in two, widely divergent ways. The first—and dominant—interpretation is activist in orientation; the American people
are seen to have the responsiblity to anticipate Christ's return by
building *themselves* "the Kingdom of God on earth." This version of
the myth has been termed "post-millennial" since Christ is expected
to return only after the earthly kingdom of God has been established. In this version, Christ may be the ruler of the kingdom, but
humankind nevertheless plays a significant role in its construction.

The second interpretation of the millennial myth, although less
popular today, was historically the earliest. According to this reading, the earth is essentially a doomed place and no amount of
human effort can make it any better. Evil is winning the battle
against good. The best anyone can do is to wait for the imminent
return of Christ to bring an end to it all in one final and irrevocable
battle—Armageddon. Despite this emphasis on the "apocalyptic"
or cataclysmic elements of the millennial myth, the people who
hold to this version are just as hopeful in their way as post-millen-
nialists. These people, too, believe that the earth will be a paradise
for a thousand years, but, importantly, they reject all collective
human efforts such as secular government to bring this paradise
about. The best you can do is to make sure that you yourself are
pure of heart and clean of soul so that despite the inevitable sufferings of the world during the coming period of transition, your
faithfulness will ultimately be rewarded with citizenship in the
millennial kingdom. Since in this version Christ's Second Coming
is seen as the necessary first step toward this thousand-year par-

adise, those who believe in it are called "pre-millennialists" or, in American parlance, "Adventists."

While it would be an anachronism to call them Adventists, the New England Puritans were actually the first representiatives of this tradition in America. The Puritans interpreted their flight to the North American continent in the early seventeenth century as an escape into the wilderness. There they would form a "remnant" of mankind which, free from the corrupting influences of Europe, would remain faithful to Christ to the bitter end of the world. The Puritans were fortified in this exile by the belief that this end would occur soon—both their own persecution in England and the social upheaval then tearing that land apart were seen as confirmatory signs of this fact. Many indeed searched scripture for clues as to the exact date of Christ's return. Confident in their ultimate— and speedy—redemption, the first generations of these first American sectarians managed to survive their wilderness ordeal.

Over time, of course, such fervid anticipation of the end was impossible to maintain. The very success of the American colonies at large seemed to contradict the notion of man's helplessness to better the world. In the early part of the eighteenth century the descendents of the Puritans underwent a period of intense soul-searching during which they began to question the legitmacy of some of their more pessimistic doctrines. The rest of the colonies as well were caught up in a ground-swell of religious enthusiasm, a groundswell which was characterized by its optimistic emphasis on the possibility for individual spiritual advancement. It was during this period—the First Great Awakening—that the once dominant pre-millennial myth gradually metamorphosed into its more optimistic post-millennial counterpart. Perhaps mankind could indeed make a positive contribution to the building of the kingdom on earth: did not the very success of the American colonies in building a new and better society in the face of daunting obstacles give at least an implicit divine sanction to such a view?

Decades later, the victory of the American colonists over the British in the Revolutionary War seemed to answer this question with a resounding yes. America was indeed heaven-blessed and destined to be the precursor of Christ's kingdom. As a result of the euphoria surrounding the colonists' victory, the optimistic post-millennial myth not only became dominant within America's Christian denominations, but in a semi-secularized form it also became a part of America's emerging mythic identity. No more would Puritan doom and gloom be tolerated; henceforth America and Americans would not be cowed by the evil of the world and passively wait for the millennial kingdom to fall from the sky. No, they would now go out and build it themselves!

The dynamism inherent in this new American mythic identity found its expression in many ways: the rise of industrialization, the creation of new technology, the building of new and bigger cities. Most importantly, however, this dynamism found an outlet in America's relentless westward expansion toward the Pacific. "Manifest Destiny" it was called: manifest because God had seemingly decreed that America was destined to occupy the entire North American continent.

Not surprisingly, in the minds of nineteenth-century Americans, the land at the end of the continent, California, played an important symbolic role in the myth of Manifest Destiny. The occupation and settlement of California represented for many the not-too-distant fulfillment of America's divine mission. During this early frontier period, California was constantly invested with millennial significance; the very name "Golden Gate," for example, harked back to the gate through which the Messiah was said to enter Jerusalem in the Last Days. A mural painted in 1865 in the rotunda of the nation's Capitol seems to make this connection explicit. Under a representation of the Golden Gate, the painter Emanuel Luetz juxtaposed these lines by Bishop Berkeley:

> Westward the course of Empire takes its way
> The first four acts already past
> A fifth shall close the drama with the day.

The millennial drama to which Bishop Berkeley referred was, of course, the history of humanity; for Luetz, however, as for many Americans, the final Empire was to be an American one, and California its millennial goal. In the following chapters, we should always bear in mind the depth of the post-millennial optimism which the majority of nineteenth-century American immigrants brought to the Golden State.

Millerites and the Rise of Adventism

Not every American was thrilled by the prospects for America's post-colonial future, however, especially at the dawn of the nineteenth century. For all its optimism, the United States was still a country in the process of forming itself. The character of her government was still being debated and her sovereignty was still being challenged. Consider how traumatic it must have been for the average citizen when the nation's Capitol was attacked and burned during the War of 1812. Consider, too, how vulnerable the predominantly agricultural American people must have felt in the face of rapid industrialization and urban growth. It was not surprising that a considerable minority still saw the future as fraught with danger and tribulations. Add to this environment yet another major religious revival—the Second Great Awakening—and you have the perfect environment for the rise of new prophets who, seizing on the anxieties of the age, parlayed their promises into new sectarian movements.

Adventism was one of these new movements. Its prophet, however, was as unlikely as his promise was old. Perhaps reacting to his own unsettling experiences during the War of 1812, William Miller, a Baptist layman from New York state, revived the old doom-and-gloom pre-millennialism of the Puritans. Although originally a theological liberal, Miller had decided after hundreds of hours of study that he had "broken the code" of the apocalyptic texts of the Bible. Christ's Second Coming would indeed literally occur before the millennium, Miller maintained, and, according to his calculations, it would come to pass in 1843.

Although a reluctant speaker, Miller nevertheless preached his promise and plan for the first time at a huge revival in Dresden, New York in 1831. Overnight, he became a sensation. Baptists, Methodists and many other denominations vied for his speaking services. Confident, yet less than charismatic, William Miller carefully ran through each minute step of his interpretation of scripture for countless audiences night after night. Each group of listeners was more enthusiastic than the last. Few had ever before heard such a detailed and seemingly sophisticated Biblical analysis, and many found themselves convinced that indeed the end was near.

Despite the popular reaction, however, it is doubtful whether Miller would have reached a national audience if it had not been for the unique possibility presented by something quite new on the American scene: mass media in the form of periodicals. Apparently Miller was content to preach his message to single congregations, and he sought and received a license from the Baptists in 1833 to do just that. In 1839, however, Miller happened to meet a certain Joshua Himes, one of those promotional geniuses for whom America was rapidly becoming famous. Impressed by Miller's calculations, Himes coaxed the reluctant prophet into co-founding a monthly journal to showcase his pre-millenial promise. Called *The Signs of the Times*, the journal quickly turned Miller's local movement into a national one. By 1840, the first national conference of "Adventists" was held in Boston and the movement was soon to have over 50,000 members nationwide. Soon, too, the mainline Protestant denominations began to notice a marked decline in attendence in their own churches. While originally non-denominational, Miller's Adventist movement was rapidly becoming converted into a sect, and, just as rapidly, the target of mainline Protestant hostility.

With the approach of 1843, millennial expectations were at a fever's pitch in America. Adventists and non-Adventists alike waited with bated breath for the final consummation of the world. In January of that year Miller upped the ante by making his original predictions more precise: "I am fully convinced," he announced in his journal, "that somewhere between March twenty-first, 1843, and March twenty-first, 1844, according to the Jewish mode of computation of time, Christ will come." Many sold off property in anticipation, or squandered their life's savings with the attitude "you can't take it with you." Most, however, waited and watched with quiet, tense expectation.

First March 21, 1843, came and went; and then March 21, 1844, passed as well. Nothing happened. Many reeled under what was soon to be called—with the sarcasm typical of the newspapers of the time—"the Great Disappointment." Miller's movement was in danger of imminent collapse. Quickly, Miller found errors in his original date calculation and he produced a new one: October 21, 1844. Again excitement mounted and again the date passed without incident. After this—the "Second Great Disappointment"—Miller threw in the towel and refused to set any more dates. Still fervent in his beliefs, but not so confident in his code-breaking abilities, the first prophet of nineteenth-century Adventism quietly retired from public life and washed his hands of the entire movement. This, however, was just the beginning.

Seventh-Day Adventists

Although many of the 50,000 Millerites returned to their original denominations, large numbers did not. Some continued to calculate new dates, while others sought to make sense of Miller's original one. Amongst the latter was a charismatic young woman named Ellen Gould Harmon who, in a vision in 1844, was told that indeed the Son of Man had returned in 1843, but in a spiritual, not material, form. Moreover, she was also told that mankind was indeed living in the Last Days, although much work had to be done before Christ would return in the flesh. Spread the Adventist message, Harmon was commanded, and take advantage of the interim between Christ's spiritual and physical return to save as many more as possible.

Due to her native charisma and strength of character—for young women did not normally occupy the pulpits of churches in the early nineteenth century—Ellen Gould Harmon nevertheless went on the road preaching her illuminist promise of Christ's spiritual coming to other receptive Adventists. In 1846, on one of her many speaking tours, Harmon met and married James White, an Adventist from Washington, New Hampshire. Together they formed a dynamic team and within a year a small group had coalesced around Ellen and James White in Washington. There, Ellen White began to formulate her plan for the revised Adventist promise, a plan which would subsequently be ratified by new visions.

Drawing on Baptist theology, Mrs. White emphasized the importance of scripture and its central role in defining Adventist beliefs. It seems that she was also influenced by many of the popular religious ideas and attitudes that happened to be current at the time. One such attitude was strongly restorationist in tone and regarded the "old law" of the Old Testament as still binding on true Christians. As a token of her respect for the "old law," Mrs. White commanded that her group return to the Saturday Sabbath. It was from this practice that the group took its name: "Seventh-Day" Adventism (often abbreviated SDA).

Along with her Old Testament restorationism, Mrs. White was also strongly influenced by many of the popular health reformers of her day. During the early part of the nineteenth century, America underwent a health craze with strong religious overtones; countless fads proliferated which were claimed to simultaneously purify body *and* soul. For Mrs. White, however, an emphasis on health was important not for life in this world, but for life in the next one. After all, the millennial kingdom was to be an earthly kingdom, and as such, only those who were pure physically as well as spiritually could expect to be admitted. Accordingly, SDA members were expected to abstain from coffee, tea, and other stimulants, as well as that American staple, tobacco. Diet was emphasized as well, and vegetarianism strongly encouraged. A variety of new foods came to be invented by the Seventh-Day Adventists, of which the most popular was a new cereal preparation called the corn flake, brain-child of an early SDA member by the name of Kellogg.

The transition from sect to church was not an easy one for Seventh-Day Adventism. Not only did hostility remain from the days of the two Great Disappointments, but the vast majority of Americans, despite the mounting frictions between North and South which would soon engulf the nation in war, were still millennial optimists. The Whites therefore encouraged SDA members to move west, assuring them that the frontier offered more fruitful opportunities for proselytization than the "Gospel-hardened" Atlantic states. In 1855 the publishing operation of the SDA moved to Battle Creek, Michigan, and soon the rest of the church organization followed, making Battle Creek the permanent SDA headquarters. By this time a definite episcopal structure had been decided upon, and a national organization—called a conference—was established. The SDA also began to open its own elementary schools in order to raise their children in an environment free from the corrupting influences of society at large.

By 1865, the sect had already become well enough established to be incorporated and recognized as an official denomination by the U.S. government, a fact which saved many SDA members from service in the last days of the Civil War. This transition from sect to church, however, began to subtly change the tone of Seventh-Day Adventism. The SDA increasingly began to take on the trappings of a mainline Protestant denomination. Although ardent pre-millennialism still remained the most distinctive doctrine of the church, the date-setting with which the movement began and from which it derived much of its energy was now actively discouraged. It was difficult, it seems, to get people interested in building an organization if the world was going to end tomorrow.

The SDA in California

From the beginning, the Seventh-Day Adventists set themselves apart from the rest of the nineteenth-century American society; their belief in the imminence of the Second Coming, their Saturday Sabbath-keeping, health consciousness, separate schools, non-involvement in government, as well as their participation in such explosive issues as abolitionism and pacifism, made them seem an alien presence. It was natural then that, like the Mormons before them, they continued to trek farther into the wilderness of the American frontier. Perhaps too, they were drawn by the millennially-tinged reputation of California. In any case, as early as 1855 an SDA member who had been lured to the gold fields around Sacramento had written back to the General Conference suggesting that the state was ready for missionization. Four years later, Merritt S. Kellogg, son of the cereal king, traveled overland to California, arriving almost penniless and without introductions amongst the muddy streets of San Francisco. Soon, however, Kellogg had encountered his first converts, and found himself holding the first Saturday Sabbath services in California in the parlor of Mr. B.G. St. John of Minna Street.

By 1865 Kellogg felt that the time was ripe for SDA expansion in the Golden State and wrote off to the General Conference for more missionaries. Three years later his request was fulfilled with the arrival of J.N. Loughborough and D.T. Bourdeau. Ministering at first to the congregation in San Francisco, the pair soon moved off to the small town of Petaluma north of the city at the behest of some local townsmen who had read about the SDA's missionary efforts in an old New York newspaper.

There in Petaluma, despite the invitation, Loughborough and Bourdeau encountered significant resistance to their message. Having arrived so shortly after the Civil War, the two missionaries found that patriotic feeling was still running high, even in faraway California, and their call for pacifism and non-involvement in government was unpopular. Moreover, the countryside of California was still a thoroughly frontier environment, filled with a rough-and-ready crowd, mostly male, and ill-disposed to give up such amusements as drinking and smoking. For most, calls to abstinence were even more intolerable than a lack of patriotism or a constant harping on Doomsday.

Nevertheless, the two missionaries did manage to convert

twenty people during a tent meeting in Petaluma, and with this nucleus they slowly expanded their efforts to other towns in Sonoma County. Within a year they had founded congregations in Windsor, Sebastopol, and Santa Rosa. It was in this last town that the first SDA baptismal service was held, and the first SDA church west of the Rockies was built, both in 1869.

By 1870 Seventh-Day Adventism counted seventy members in Sonoma County. J.N. Loughborough had since returned to the original congregation in San Francisco, and shortly the Sonoma and San Francisco congregations had formed a unified state organization, electing Bourdeau as its president. In its enthusiasm, one of the state organization's first orders of business was to invite the founding couple of SDA to come see the wonders of California. Their enthusiasm must have been contagious since, after a long and dangerous overland trek, Ellen and James White arrived in Windsor, Sonoma County, in October of 1872. Their visit solidified the ties between the General Conference and the California Seventh-Day Adventists. By 1873, the General Conference had raised the California state organization to conference status.

The 1870s was a decade of growth for Seventh-Day Adventism in the Golden State. D.T. Bourdeau, who continued in the office of president until 1878, had decided to move the offices of the California conference to Oakland, thus making this city the hub of SDA missionization for the state. Missionaries soon founded new congregations in the north, in Red Bluff and the Napa Valley; to the south, in Hollister and Gilroy; and to the east, in the San Joaquin Valley. Moses J. Church, known as the father of Fresno, was an ardent Seventh-Day Adventist who actively used his Fresno-based newspaper to spread the new faith throughout the Valley.

It was not too long after that that Seventh-Day Adventism made its appearance in Southern California. In 1874, John B. Judson became the first active Adventist in the Los Angeles area. Soon, a congregation was formed in San Pasqual Valley, and later SDA churches could be found in Norwalk (1874), San Diego, San Pedro, and Pasadena (all circa 1875), and then in Los Angeles itself (1879). California also became the jumping off point for SDA missionaries to other states (Nevada, Arizona), as well as for international missionary efforts to the Hawaiian Islands, China, Fiji, and South Africa.

Institutionally as well, SDA continued to expand in California during the 1870s. In 1876, the first Adventist Bible Institute was set up in Oakland in order to train missionaries. The first classes were personally conducted by the Whites themselves. This would be the first of many educational institutions created in California under the auspices of SDA. The business side of the church was not neglected either; in response to a prophecy by his wife, James White began publishing an Adventist newspaper, *The Signs of the Times*, in Oakland in 1874. In time this would blossom into the Pacific Seventh-Day Adventist Publishing Association, a corporation that survives to this day.

Throughout the 1870s and '80s, California was a rapidly changing society. Frontier conditions had been replaced by regular town life, and better communications had brought the state's culture more into alignment with the rest of the Union. Immigrants were now less likely to be rootless young men looking to get rich quick, but families looking to settle. This change was reflected in the propaganda produced by civic boosters in L.A. and San Francisco in order to entice people to California; instead of wealth, health was stressed, and endless pages were written in praise of California's Mediterranean climate. Soon, along with the families came older, retired midwesterners who, having grown rich tilling the prairie soil, now sought to escape the rigors of that life in sunny, healthy California.

The shift from wealth to health aided somewhat the California growth of Seventh-Day Adventism in the last decades of the nineteenth century. Although SDA health concerns had been a liability just scant decades before, the emphasis on bodily well-being now became a drawing card. Accordingly, the SDA dedicated large sums of money to institutional expressions of its health focus; in 1878, the church opened the Rural Health Retreat in Sonoma Valley which, under the capable direction of the multi-talented Merritt G. Kellogg, soon became the St. Helena Sanitarium and Hospital. In conjunction with the Health Retreat, the SDA began to publish the *Pacific Health Journal and Temperance Advocate*, a periodical which lives on today as *Life and Health*. The promoting of health foods also became a growing concern. Farms, small factories and restaurants, all devoted to the production and distribution of health food, were created. The first vegetarian restaurant in California was opened by E. G. Fulton and M. A. Hollister in San Diego around 1886; and in Los Angeles, a second vegetarian restaurant was opened in conjunction with a medical treatment facility under the direction of Dr. Moran a year later.

Despite these tactical moves, however, overall growth of Seventh-Day Adventism slowed by the 1890s. Paradoxically, part of the reason was due to some of the same factors which caused the health boom in California in the first place: immigration from the Midwest. Many of these immigrants, despite their desire to escape the climate of the Midwest, remained nevertheless extremely loyal culturally to their home states. In Southern California especially this meant the wholesale transplantation of mainline Protestantism and its institutions. By the late 1880s Los Angeles and its environs had come to be controlled by Episcopalians, Lutherans, Congregationalists, and Methodists. Thus while the SDA's health orientation still remained attractive well into the twentieth century, the church's pre-millennialism became increasingly out of place against the backdrop of mainline Protestant post-millennial optimism of the century's first two decades. Moreover, as we shall see in the next chapter, other health-oriented sectarian movements such as Christian Science would shortly challenge the SDA in California.

Unlike some of the other sectarian movements we will explore in this volume, Seventh-Day Adventism actually had only limited success in the early days of California. By 1885 the SDA California Conference had a membership of just 1,587, a figure which grew but slowly in the next two decades. After the death of James White in 1881, Ellen White decided to return to Battle Creek from California. Perhaps she sensed that cultural changes in the West had made it more difficult to gain adherents to her promise. More likely, however, Mrs. White was alarmed by the rise of a new Adventist prophet in the East, a prophet whose promise more closely resembled the original Adventist promise of William Miller, and whose plan would soon cause a similar millennial uproar.

The Rise of the Jehovah's Witnesses

As we mentioned in the introductory chapters of this volume, sectarian movements are often responses to the rigidification of a church, and thus it is not surprising to find that as sects like SDA made the transition to church, they in turn generated new sectarian groups. Such was the case in the late nineteenth century with the arrival of the third great Adventist movement, the Jehovah's Witnesses.

The prophet of this new sectarian movement was Charles Taze Russell. Russell, the son of a wealthy furniture store owner from Philadelphia, had been in his youth an ardent Adventist and follower of a group much like Ellen G. White's SDA. Later in life, however, Russell came to be influenced by the debate then raging between the "Modernists," theological liberals who accepted higher biblical criticism, and the theological conservatives. Like the conservatives of today, the Fundamentalists of the late nineteenth century rejected all allegorizing of the Bible, arguing that anything less than a literal reading of scripture was to doubt the word of God. For Charles Taze Russell, a confirmed Adventist and conservative, this assertion cast grave doubts on the claim that Christ's Second Coming in 1843 could have been anything other than in the flesh. Obviously the 1843 date touted by the "spiritualizing" Adventists was wrong. The apocalyptic code of the Bible still remained to be broken.

Russell's promise was again a proclamation of Christ's imminent return, and his plan consisted of yet a new key to apocalyptic code. Taking his cue from "dispensationalism"—a new schema for history based on the Book of Daniel and a combination of biblical precedents—Russell calculated that the real Advent would occur in 1914. In addition to this end date, Russell also declared that the year 1874 had marked the beginning of what he called the "millennial dawn:" an era in which marvelous things would happen in anticipation of the end. The Jews, for example, would return to Palestine, and all secular governments would be overthrown in preparation for the Lord's arrival. This interim was also the last opportunity for the word of God to be preached before the world witnessed Armageddon, that final terrible battle between good and evil in which all the unconverted "heathens" would be destroyed. Like Mrs. White's SDA before him, Russell saw the responsibility for this last conversion campaign as the divinely appointed duty of his new sect, which he called the "Millennial Dawn Bible Students." Unlike the SDA, however, Russell also taught that salvation, even for the Bible Students, was contingent; among those living during the forty-year "millennial dawn" period, only those who accepted Russell's promise *and* actively preached it would be saved and escape the sufferings and tribulations of the coming apocalypse.

Many of Russell's distinctive doctrines can be traced back to his literal biblicism. One such doctrine—that of the two classes of believers—was the fruit of an exceptionally close reading of the Bible. In Russell's interpretation of Revelation the faithful remnant will be divided into two groups at the close of Christ's thousand-year reign on earth: a "heavenly class," which will rule with Christ in heaven, and an "earthly class," which will remain on earth and serve those above. According to Revelation 7:4-9, the heavenly class will be limited to 144,000. Most of these, Russell speculated, had already lived during Jesus' day, but some, perhaps as many as 10,000, were living still. Amongst the Bible Students, therefore, there was active competition to demonstrate one's "heavenly" status through proselytization, although, of course, only God knew who was "to be in that number."

While a visionary, Charles Taze Russell was also an intensely practical man and saw no reason to confine his preaching to a single pulpit. Accordingly, in July of 1879, Russell followed in the footsteps of William Miller and Joshua Himes and began to spread his promise and plan by means of a new journal specifically targeted at the most receptive audience. Using a subscription list acquired from another Adventist publication, Russell sent out 6,000 free copies of his *Zion's Watchtower and Herald of Christ's Presence* to Adventists around the country. Thus Russell's movement, as one scholar put it, essentially began as a mail-order religion; the time was ripe, however, for both the medium and the message. A year later, many small congregations, called ecclesiae, began to gather on a regular basis for group readings of Russell's magazine. In 1881 Russell moved to regularize communication with these ecclesiae through his newly incorporated Zion's Watchtower and Bible Tract Society. Soon, this mail-order prophet found himself the president of a huge administrative and publishing empire centered in Brooklyn, New York, and devoted exclusively to the propagation of the Russellite promise and plan.

From that point until his death, Russell divided his time between recording his prophecies—his collected works ran over several dozen volumes—and tending to the further growth and consolidation of his movement. At first the various congregations of Bible Students were only loosely affiliated with the Brooklyn headquarters. They maintained their connection through subscription to the *Watchtower* and other periodicals Russell produced. Soon, however, they were being visited by a paid Brooklyn representative—called a pilgrim—who would encourage the ecclesiae to support the main office by selling Russell's literature to neighbors and friends. A wide variety of sale techniques were introduced in this way, including the use of portable phonographs and motion pictures. Russell, despite his undeniable sincerity and commitment to his prophetic mission, was nevertheless a businessman at heart, and knew that no organization survived unless it stood on firm financial footing. Indeed, it was probably the commercial inertia of the Watchtower Society which helped Russell's movement survive the two impending crises which would have broken lesser sectarian movements.

The coincidence of 1914 with the outbreak of World War I was a cause for elation amongst Russell's Bible Students. It appeared to many to herald the onset of Armageddon. Russell's followers waited in tense expectation for Christ's arrival, just as Miller's followers had decades before. Many Bible Students sold property and prepared for the end, and the movement gained adherents on a daily basis. As the war dragged on, however, Russell, like Miller, was forced to do what any self-respecting prophet dreads doing: he admitted he was in error and calculated a new date: 1916. Suddenly and unexpectedly, however, Russell died on October 31, 1916. The movement was thrown into turmoil. Just as the years 1843 and 1844 had been the two "Great Disappointments" of the Millerites, 1914 and 1916 were to have the same connotations for the Millennial Dawn Bible Students.

Despite these setbacks, a number of factors helped not only to keep the movement alive but also enthusiastic and growing. As we mentioned above, before he died Russell had built a solid organization around the publication and distribution of his promise, an organization which had become immensely profitable from the turn of the century on. Russell had also carefully anointed a successor whose pragmatic charisma approximated Russell's own. "Judge" Joseph Rutherford was a lawyer and some-time judge from Morgan County, Missouri. First introduced to Russell's teachings when he was visited in his law offices by several Bible Students in 1894, Rutherford formally joined the movement in 1906, and soon became Russell's trusted legal advisor. By the time Russell died in 1916, Rutherford was ready to step in as president of the Watchtower Society.

The wisdom of Russell's choice of successor was quickly

proven. By all accounts Judge Rutherford was a flamboyant and pugnacious character who relished a good fight—whether theological or physical. Both of these qualities were severely tested when the judge and other leaders of the Watchtower Society were arrested and imprisoned by the Federal government on trumped-up charges of treason in 1917. This was the period of America's entry into World War I, and the militant pacifism of the Bible Students was a thorn in the side of a particularly sensitive administration. Released in 1919 after all the charges had been dropped, Rutherford came to be seen as a martyr within the Millennial Dawn movement and his prestige grew. He began to don the prophetic mantle as Russell's spiritual heir, and to make what he claimed were inspired pronouncements correcting some of the former prophet's teachings. Soon, a new series of apocalyptic dates began to flow from Rutherford's pen.

The judge quickly and confidently imposed his stamp on this burgeoning sectarian movement. It was Rutherford's decision to change the name of the movement to the Jehovah's Witnesses (after a passage in Isaiah 43:11, "ye are my witnesses saith Jehovah, and my servants whom I have chosen."). Rutherford also introduced significant changes in doctrine and structure. After 1919, the relationship between the Brooklyn headquarters and the ecclesiae became rigidly hierarchical and autocratic; soon all local property was owned by the Society, and individual congregations came to exercise less and less independence. By 1938, all meetings and services were scripted by the Brooklyn headquarters such that on any given day the same texts were used in every "Kingdom Hall."

Like many Adventist groups, strict separation from society at large was an important aspect of the Witness belief structure. Under Rutherford's watch such segregation was even more stringently insisted upon and became a hallmark of the sect. Rigid conformity had come to be expected from all Witness members, and questioning of the central hierarchy was discouraged. In 1929 Witnesses were explicitly told to obey the Watchtower Society above any earthly government, and in the case of conflict, the Society's word was to be a law above all others. Witnesses were taught that they should strive to put themselves above national or other allegiances, and beyond the reach of any political power. Because of this demand—and the willingness of thousands of individual Witnesses to comply with it—the Jehovah's Witnesses has come to have the dubious distinction of being the religious sect which, by far, has been the most frequently challenged in courts of law during the present century.

Rutherford also instituted what would become the most distinctive feature of the Jehovah's Witnesses: door-to-door proselytization. Claiming that the 144,000 saints had all been sealed in 1914, Judge Rutherford reemphasized that all new members, now relegated to the earthly class, could easily jeopardize their salvation if they failed to reach just one potential convert before the end. Moreover, while eventually discouraging further date-setting, Rutherford nevertheless maintained that, based on Matthew 24:14, the Advent would occur at the moment when everyone on the planet had heard the Gospel message. Thus, every individual Witness was made an active minister, and since 1940, direct door-to-door preaching has been stressed above all other methods of proselytization.

The dedicated Witness takes these preaching duties extremely seriously, as does the central organization its international missionary efforts. Today, the Jehovah's Witnesses are active in over 211 countries with 66,000 congregations. Moreover, in each of these countries the Watchtower Society has produced a translation of the Bible in the local language and script.

The First Appearance of the Jehovah's Witnesses in California

Although it seems likely that the Jehovah's Witnesses had reached California in the guise of Russell's Millennial Dawn Bible Students as early as the 1880s, the first definitive evidence we have of an ecclesia in the Golden State comes shortly before Russell's death in 1916. Russell relished debate and greatly enjoyed preaching his promise and plan to large public gatherings. In the 1890s he began a series of whistle-stop tours across the country, eventually winding up all such tours in Los Angeles. Here, he was an immensely popular speaker. It is reported that one of Russell's lectures attracted a crowd of over 12,000 to the downtown Trinity Auditorium. It is not surprising therefore that we hear of a small congregation forming in Los Angeles during the early teens of this century. In fact, it appears that this was the last ecclesia to hear the words of the prophet, for a day after visiting the Los Angeles group, Russell collapsed and died on the train trip back to New York.

Judge Rutherford maintained the California connection, but in a way that underscored both his literal biblicism and California's indelible millennial associations. Prison had left Rutherford unbowed in spirit but very much the worse for wear in terms of his health. Accordingly, his doctors advised him to go west to recover, and, naturally enough, when "health" was associated with the West, it meant California. From 1919 on, Rutherford wintered in San Diego, first staying at the Hotel Coronado, and then purchasing a small home in town. Later, in 1929, Rutherford moved permanently to San Diego, having constructed there a huge Spanish-style mansion, which he christened *Beth Sarim* (Hebrew for "House of the Princes"). According to a *Time* magazine article of the day, Rutherford justified the move to California because he felt that the Old Testament prophets (whose return would herald the Advent), would feel more at home both before and after the event in the semi-tropical environment of the California coast. The kingdom after all was to be an earthly paradise, and California most closely approximated what the judge thought that paradise would be like. It was at *Beth Sarim* that Rutherford finally died in 1942, and it was there that he wished to be buried.

While Witnesses today smile at Rutherford's eccentricities—the pre-Advent return of the Old Testament prophets, for example, is no longer current teaching—the Witnesses nevertheless wholeheartedly agree with the need for practical preparation for the coming millennium. The Witnesses, for example, see their local church structures as more than just meeting places. "Kingdom Halls" are so called because Witnesses believe that these will be the only structures left standing after Armageddon; as such, they will form the nucleus of hundreds of millennial cities. Kingdom Halls will, in a sense, serve as the "city halls" for these cities, and detailed plans for post-apocalyptic local government are ready and waiting for that fateful day when the Witnesses find themselves in sole possession of the world.

With the death of Rutherford, the leadership of the Watchtower Society moved back to New York. Since the bulk of the Watchtower operations had remained in the East, this return was motivated by sheer administrative practicality. Nevertheless, another and perhaps just as potent reason for the return back east was that, for all of Russell's and Rutherford's enthusiasm for California, the Witnesses during their first years in the state never approached even the SDA's modest success in recruiting members. A perusal of the 1940 Los Angeles telephone directory reveals only two Kingdom Halls for the entire L.A. basin. What's more, the Witnesses had also been the targets of unremitting hostility ever since their arrival into the state. California had just not been the fertile ground for the pre-millennial promise as the first two Witness prophets had thought it would be.

Apparently, both the timing and the location of the Witnesses' early efforts in the state severely restricted the possibilities for success. In contrast to the SDA, which had established itself in Northern California after the Civil War, the Watchtower Society had only begun to be active in the state some fifty years later, and then mainly in the South. The sociocultural differences between the two halves of California during these two periods was vast. Granted there was hostility from the mainline Protestant denominations toward the SDA in Northern California, but the denominations did not have the political power nor cultural clout in the mid-nineteenth century to do this sectarian movement much harm. In fact, in the early 1880s the SDA spearheaded a successful drive to repeal the Sunday Sabbath laws which were fiercely championed by the mainline denominations but were blasphemous to Saturday Sabbatarians.

In the Southland, however, especially in Los Angeles, the mainline Protestant denominations had, by the first decades of the twentieth century, formed themselves into a formidable cultural and political force. Acting as a bloc, the mainline denominations now did not hesitate to vigorously enforce their American-led, post-millennial vision of the future. Thus we find the Jehovah's Witnesses constantly being harassed in Los Angeles, usually with the justification that the movement was unpatriotic and subversive. After one of Rutherford's lectures was printed verbatim on the front page of the *Los Angeles Tribune* in February, 1918, for example, the local clergy objected strongly and vociferously and called for a statewide boycott of the paper. A week later, perhaps taking advantage of the current wave of hostility against the group, the Army Intelligence Bureau seized the Witnesses' Los Angeles office, citing a long-standing accusation of espionage and disloyalty as the reason for their raid. Such treatment of Witnesses was typical. For all of California's vaunted reputation for tolerance, it seems that the Jehovah's Witnesses' vision of paradise was one which many Californians of that time and place found impossible to accept.

A Postscript to the History of Adventism in California

By World War II, both the Seventh-Day Adventists and the Jehovah's Witnesses had become common features in the religious landscape of America. And yet, while the SDA has enjoyed respectable, but not spectacular growth, the Jehovah's Witnesses' increases in membership both nationally and internationally has been spectacular indeed. Moreover, while accurate membership statistics for the Witnesses are hard to come by, if the increase in Kingdom Halls is any indication (from two in the entire Los Angeles basin in the '40s to twenty-seven in the downtown area alone today), their growth has been even more spectacular in California than almost anywhere else in the country. In light of the inauspicious beginnings of the movement in the state, we could well ask, what has changed?

Beginning in the 1960s many Americans again began to question the validity of the nation's mythic post-millennial underpinnings. A combination of political, economic and environmental crises shook peoples' faith in the efficacy and wisdom of their institutions. Watergate, Vietnam, and the OPEC oil embargo of the seventies all contributed to create a climate of anxiety, a climate which the threat of global nuclear war only intensified. For many, optimism in the future was gradually coming to be replaced by pessimism.

California was especially hard-hit by this fundamental mood-shift. As the preeminent symbol of America's post-millennial project, California's problems became emblematic of the larger national malaise. It is not surprising therefore that sectarian groups which claimed to make sense of this malaise would become popular; it is also not surprising that the pre-millennial perspective, which sees in tribulations signs of the coming paradise, would be in the forefront of such groups. Obviously many Californians, having watched their own earthly paradise begin to fade, have responded with enthusiasm to the Witness promise of an imminent new one.

SOURCES AND FURTHER READING

Albanese, Catherine L. *America: Religions and Religion.* Belmont, Ca.: Wadsworth Publishing Co., 1981.

Frankiel, Sandra Sizer. *California's Spiritual Frontiers: Religious Alternatives in Anglo-Protestantism, 1850-1910.* Berkeley: University of California Press, 1988.

Land, Gary (ed.) *Adventism in America: A History.* Grand Rapids, Mich.: William B. Eerdmans Publishing Co., 1986.

Melton, J. Gordon. *The Encyclopedia of American Religions,* 3rd edition. Detroit: Gale Research, 1989.

Singleton, Gregory. *Religion in the City of Angeles: American Protestant Culture and Urbanization, Los Angeles, 1850-1930.* Ann Arbor: UMI Research Press, 1979.

5 Christian Science and New Thought in California: Seeking Health, Happiness and Prosperity in Paradise

During the Pacific-Panama International Exposition held in San Francisco in 1915, Saturday, August 28 was officially declared "New Thought Day." On a typically gorgeous, sunny morning on the Exposition grounds, while presenting a medal commemorating the occasion, Mr. James A. Edgerton, president of the International New Thought Alliance, made the following comments:

> Mrs. Annie Rix Militz, as representing the California New Thought Exposition Committee, referred to this California sunshine as New Thought weather. While it is perfectly true that New Thought stands for mental sunshine, we are entirely willing to give God and your wonderful climate out here some of the credit for this perfect day, but ask you to note the one fact, that New Thought flourishes most where physical and spiritual sunshine abound, as is proven by its strength upon the Golden Coast. I believe our Cause is stronger in California than in any other part of the world. New Thought is an attempt to express California weather in our lives (*Master Mind*, Vol. IX, 50).

Mr. Edgerton was right. Christian Science and New Thought, two nineteenth-century sectarian religions that embrace a "mind over matter," positive-thinking philosophy, simply worked better in the gentle climate of California. These metaphysical religions and California were meant for each other, as though California represented a kind of exterior assurance that inner, psychological affirmations of health, happiness, and prosperity were attuned with cosmic harmony. California was an outer manifestation of inner abundance; a place where the possibilites were endless.

Before meeting our prophets in the "metaphysical movement"—Mary Baker Eddy in Christian Science and leaders such as Emma Curtis Hopkins, Malinda Cramer, Annie Rix Militz, Charles Fillmore, and Ernest Holmes in the more diversified New Thought movement—it is necessary to make a few general remarks about this worldview in relationship to American culture, noting again in sectarian religions the neat coincidence between place, promise, and possibility. We might best approach the constellation of ideas that make up the metaphysical worldview by using the religio-cultural characteristics discussed in chapter two: Perfectionism, Universalism, Illuminism, and Millennialism.

The broad descriptive term, "metaphysical," used as a general category for these religions, is our entrance into understanding perfectionism as an emerging force in Christian Science and New Thought. While both groups engage a type of philosophical Idealism, "metaphysical" is not used in a manner common to the trained philosopher. Rather it denotes the primacy of Mind as *the* controlling factor in human experience. As we will see, major differences exist between Christian Science and New Thought, but at the heart of the metaphysical perspective is the theological/ontological affirmation that God is perfect Mind, and human beings, in reality, exist as a perfect manifestation of that Divine Mind. The implications of metaphysical perfectionism are nicely summarized in Mary Baker Eddy's "Scientific Statement of Beings:"

> There is no life, truth, intelligence nor substance in matter. All is infinite Mind and its infinite manifestation, for God is All-in-All. Spirit is immortal truth; matter is mortal error. Spirit is the real and eternal; matter is the unreal and temporal. Spirit is God, and man is His image and likeness. Therefore man is not material; he is spiritual (*Science and Health*, pg. 468).

If God is Mind and the substance of being is Spirit, then "man," as the perfect reflection or expression of Mind can be, must be, as perfect as God. It is not some kind of "original sin" that causes human beings to experience suffering, lack, and death but negative thinking! As the "image and likeness of God," humans exist as the expression of God's own being.

Though at the opposite end of the metaphysical spectrum from the Mormon material universe, the same universalist freedom exists in Christian Science and New Thought. All human beings have access to the power of Divine Mind, and this power, properly used, brings unlimited health, happiness, and prosperity. Thus, once again, we see the very practical nature of nineteenth-century sectarian religions. One does not pray to a whimsical, distant, "old man in the sky" for health, happiness, and prosperity. These are qualities of God's unchanging expression. God, as Divine Principle, can be demonstrated, *scientifically*, by anyone who knows and affirms this principle of being. The "can-do" spirit of a country intoxicated with democratic ideals, finds religious form in a salvation available to anyone who plugs into mind power. By turning the mental dial from the limited, material channel, to the unlimited spiritual one, everyone has immediate access, experientially, to God. To perceive the universe as matter is an error in thinking which, at best, turns life into a rollercoaster journey of pleasure and pain, joy and suffering, lack and abundance. Since thoughts scientifically control experience, positive thinking could absolutely be relied on to produce positive experiences. And, as we shall see, it was just a bit easier to demonstrate health, if not prosperity, in the "golden glow" of California culture.

For the prophets of the metaphysical movements, this new light, illuminism, could be expressed in millennial terms or seen as eternal. Certainly, Divine Mind and its expression were an eternal, unchanging reality. But, from the limited, mortal perspective, this "new understanding" inaugurated a "new age," a gift from America to the world, or even the Second Coming of Christ prophesied by Jesus himself. With very few exceptions, nineteenth-century metaphysical leaders plugged into the prevailing Christian mythos but only on their own terms. The Bible was in need of "spiritual interpretation" which would unlock the real import of scripture. In fact, Mary Baker Eddy's textbook, *Science and Health with Key to the Scriptures*, set the trend for this type of interpretive effort.

Invariably, Jesus was seen not as a unique savior who atoned for human sin, as traditional Christianity taught but, the first human being to understand and fully express Divine Mind. The real lesson of the Gospels finds Jesus as exemplar—a human being who attained Christ consciousness and was then, scientifically, able to demonstrate mastery of sin, disease, and death. Once illuminated, the metaphysical perspective took on millennial overtones especially when empowered by the key elements of the American culture core.

As we found in the Mormon saga, metaphysicians saw themselves as a people prepared by God in a new land and destined to reveal "Truth." For the Christian Scientist or New Thoughter, health, wealth, and happiness represented qualities of God that are scientifically demonstrable for human beings to know that they reflect the Divine Mind. This metaphysical ideal finds social expression in that concept loosely described as the "Protestant work ethic"—simply put, "Think positively, work hard, maintain the status quo, and all things shall be added unto you."

Another important observation that needs to be made is the distinctly feminist roots of Christian Science and New Thought. Charles Fillmore, one of the founders of Unity School of Christianity, and Ernest Holmes, founder of Religious Science, are two important figures who certainly play major roles in the metaphysical saga. But, as we will see, the real "movers and shakers" in the movement are women. In fact, the early years of the metaphysical movement can only be understood as a religious manifestation of a social phenomenon that was reshaping life in the United States during the later years of the nineteenth century: women's clubs, women's political organizations, women, in general, joining together to confront the intellectual and cultural challenges of the 1880s and 1890s and reform what they conceived to be a degenerating social order.

Christian Science and New Thought organizations were seen as part of this struggle. Writing in an early New Thought journal, *Christian Science Thought*, Helen Wilmans, a well-known women's rights activist of her time declared,

> It is a noticeable fact that the Mental or Christian Science movement is a woman's movement. It may not be apparent to the casual observer, but it is nevertheless true, that in this movement woman's real voice has been heard for the first time in the history of the race (June 1890).

At one level, women, no doubt, gravitated toward the Christian Science movement because these religious organizations represented alternative avenues toward status and power in a male-dominated society. Certainly the late Victorian period was one of nascent feminism, and alternative women's roles were an important part of the beliefs and practices of Pentecostal and Holiness movements, Adventist groups, as well as Christian Science, Theosophy, and New Thought. The Victorian image of women was one of stifling domesticity, and a woman was often reduced to being just an ornament in the home, a bauble testifying to her husband's social status.

However, at a deeper level, the rise of feminist religion in the form of our metaphysical religions has less to do with a grab for alternative sources of power and more to do with the fact that women were attuned to changing religious/psychological needs at a time when American society was undergoing drastic social transformation. In other words, because women were marginalized—cut off from normal avenues of achievement—they were better able to respond to social change while the male perspective remained encrusted in an orthodox Calvinist worldview which was rapidly becoming an existential and theological vacuum to a large number of American citizens who possessed even remote concerns about the religious dimension of human existence.

We are speaking here of the social revolution, described in chapter two, as the agrarian/small town extended family began to break up in the diversifying atmosphere of urbanization and industrialization. Women who took up professional careers found themselves torn between old expectations of marriage and children and the growing possibility of carving out a niche in the daily functions of an increasingly complex cultural environment. In addition, the new stress on "science" resonated comfortably with a traditional women's role—that of healer in the family setting. It made perfect sense that a distinctly woman's religion would combine scientific practicality with the nurturing aspect of healing. Once again, we see that remarkable connection between the emergence of nineteenth-century sectarian religion and the alignment of contributing factors in the cultural environment.

When we focus our historical aperture on the bustling state of California in the later years of the nineteenth century, the cultural alignment becomes even more beneficial to the popular expansion of Christian Science and New Thought. One might accurately say that, like the gold rush a generation earlier, a "health" rush brought waves of immigrants to California, particularly Southern California, during the years 1870-1900. By the 1920s, California could easily be labeled the "Metaphysical Capital of the World," out-stripping the cultural centers in the East where the movement first caught fire. Theological and ecclesiastical differences aside, the stories of Christian Science and New Thought growth in California are so intertwined that it behooves us to sort out prophet, promise, plan, possibility, and place by taking these two metaphysical movements together.

Christian Science and New Thought:
Historical Background

Prophets are prone to claim that their revelation is unique. But one lesson we learn from studying nineteenth-century sectarian religions is that a successful prophet is one who profits from popular religious sentiments already existing in the spiritual imagination of the citizenry. Mid-nineteenth-century America was certainly in an experimental mood, and there was no dearth of alternative religious perspectives. Mesmerism and Swedenborgianism together implanted in the American spiritual imagination the connection between physical and psychological vitality and spiritual awareness. Emanuel Swedenborg (1688-1771), the extraordinary Swedish visionary, in voluminous writings, taught that the Divine and the natural are consubstantial in God and Man. Everything that exists visibly, in day-to-day experience, reflects patterns laid out in the spiritual world and is the end product of spiritual force.

If Swedenborgianism offered a unitive view of existence, Franz Anton Mesmer (1734-1815) provided the very principle interconnecting the human and spiritual realms: "animal magnetism," a subtle, universal substance that when properly manipulated could give life and vitality to the dying and sick. Both teachings stressed that one's relationship toward nature, society, and God depended upon attunement to the harmonizing emanations from the highest realm, Spirit of Mind. In a world that preceded the great wars between science and religion, and amongst people who had been raised to view earthly phenomena through a practical common-sense aperture, Swedenborg and Mesmer gave scientific validity to their quest for self-understanding and religious assurance.

Emersonian Transcendentalism added to this "can-do" vitality; immanence, individualism, intuition, imagination became qualities of life designed to pierce the restricting shell of materiality and usher the initiate into direct contact with the Oversoul. And Spiritualism, as we will see in a future chapter, underscored the possibility of access to other realms by creating the first toll-free connection to those who had shuffled off this mortal coil.

Perhaps no one had more influence on Mary Baker Eddy than Phineas Parkhurst Quimby (1802-66). Quimby was a blacksmith's son born in Lebanon, New Hampshire, who later became a successful clockmaker in Belfast, Maine. In 1838, while attending a lecture by the French mesmerist, Charles Poyen, Quimby underwent his first "ecstatic" revelation and gave up his clockmaking career to become a successful mesmerist and healer. In time, however, Quimby began to suspect that the healings he produced were caused by more than a manipulation of "magnetic fluids." Animal magnetism alone could not be accountable for his enormous healing success. In a flash of spiritual insight, he became convinced that it was not a physical process at all but the confidence the healer inspired in his patient and the accompanying expectation of recovery—Mind over material conditions.

Quimby, then, launched a completely new healing ministry based on an integration of scientifically demonstrable mind healing and Christian teachings. It was Quimby who first came up with the term for God, "Divine Mind." He went on to teach that the Christ was the spirit of God in all of us and a channel, when properly attuned, for ailing humans to connect to emanations of health, happiness, prosperity, and abundance. Limited, material thinking produced limited experience; spiritual thought generated abundance. Historians of religion continue to debate the question of whether Quimby should rightfully be considered the "founder" of a "Christian Science" and, thus, the intellectual and spiritual source of the New Thought movement. Quimby was not formally educated and left no comprehensive writings on his philosophy. In fact, it would fall to prolific writers such as Warren Felt Evans and Julius and Horatio Dresser to popularize Quimby's teachings. But from our perspective, what is most important about Quimby is that, in October of 1862, he treated an invalid who, once miraculously healed, would go on to found the First Church of Christ, Scientist: Mary Baker Eddy (1821-1910).

The story of Mary Baker Eddy's life and her extraordinary accomplishment in carving an enduring religious organization out of a male-dominated society is well-documented. Though it is not necessary to retell the fascinating story of her rise to metaphysical stardom, a few key milestones in her life should be noted. Born on a farm in Bow Township, near Concord, New Hampshire, this imaginative but emotionally tormented child would grow into an adulthood that, until her meeting with Quimby, was a study in misery—sickness, bad and broken marriages, and emotional disturbances which turned her life into an unceasing quest for mental and physical health. The short respite of peace she enjoyed while studying with Quimby was shattered by his death in 1866. However, following her own miraculous healing after a fall on the ice—just a few months after Quimby's demise—she became convinced that her purpose in life was to reveal the truth of Christian Science. For the next nine years, she thought, wrote, and lived in poverty, percolating her plan and promise. Eighteen seventy-five is a pivotal year in the metaphysical movement because, not only did Mrs. Eddy (as her devotees refer to her) establish the first "Christian Scientists Home" in Lynn, Massachusetts, but she published the first edition of her textbook, *Science and Health*.

By this time, Mrs. Eddy claimed for her work absolute and unique revelation. To this day, ink continues to be spilled over contesting opinions as to the source of Christian Science, many claiming that Mrs. Eddy whole-handedly borrowed her teachings and healing methods from Quimby. Others look to Warren Felt Evans as the intellectual, if not spiritual, fountainhead. For our purposes, it is acceptable to view the beginnings of the entire metaphysical movement as a dynamic merging and separating of three streams: the prophetic teachings of Quimby, as interpreted and elaborated by Evans and the Dressers; Mrs. Eddy's organizational genius which created the Christian Science movement; and the New Thought apostates who left Mrs. Eddy's movement due to the restrictive nature of her organization. In fact, the entire metaphysical movement owes Mrs. Eddy a two-fold debt. First, she had the skill and motivation to create a centrally controlled religious organization without rival in the rigidity of its restraints upon branch churches and members. In essence, it was Mrs. Eddy who first institutionalized the metaphysical promise and plan. Unlike later New Thought organizations, which developed many independent organizations, the Church of Christ, Scientist remained one unfractured institution with the center being the Mother Church in Boston and all other churches relegated to satellite status revolving around the institutional sun. This is one major difference that exists to this day between Christian Science and New Thought.

Also unlike the more eclectic New Thoughters, Christian Scientists were given little theological/intellectual tether with which to explore and claim their own metaphysical universes. Church services were guided not by independent preachers but by "readers" who were constrained to read the Bible and interpretive passages from *Science and Health* without injecting their own personal interpretations or inviting discussion. The ambitious who felt compelled to heal could only attain the status of "practitioner" (as healers were called in the movement) by studying Mrs. Eddy's writings and attending only her classes. In a way, Mrs. Eddy exhibited paradoxical tendencies as a prophet. With grandly sweeping, Victorian-laced prose, she outlined a metaphysical cosmos replete with unlimited freedom and abundance. New Thought apostates embraced this side of her teachings. On the other hand, perhaps due to a strict Calvinist upbringing, she also manifested a macabre obsession with "mortal mind." This was her terminology for the errors of limited, material thinking, and, often, mortal mind took on a persona of its own akin to a menacing, diabolical, mental assassin. Thus, Mrs. Eddy was quick to excommunicate any talented student who dared to expand the boundaries of the movement, organizationally or spiritually. In a back-handed way, this is the second debt owed to Mrs. Eddy by the general metaphysical movement. Of the many talented women who suffered the indignity of excommunication, Emma Curtis Hopkins, who once was so close to the Leader that she was editor of the *Christian Science Journal* for a year, went on to found the "Christian Science Theological Seminary" and become "teacher of teachers" in the New Thought movement. Since most of these illuminaries in the metaphysical movement had primary influence in California, let us turn to the Golden State as we chronicle the fevered quest for perfection in paradise that swept the state.

The California Story

The quest for perfection in paradise brought Christian Scientists and New Thoughters to the Golden State in the great waves of migration during the 1880s. Both movements enjoyed immediate success. By 1890, California had the third largest Christian Science membership of any state in the nation as New Thought leaders such as Malinda Cramer and Annie Rix Militz were busy organizing metaphysical alternatives.

For anyone who has lived in California, it soon becomes evident that, though the Golden State is one political entity, there are major cultural differences between the northern and southern sections of the state. This sociological reality adds spice to our story of the development of metaphysics on the coast, in that Christian Science and New Thought were successful in two quite different cultures.

In Northern California, the problems faced by America in the turbulent latter decades after the Civil War were intensified, especially in San Francisco. The multi-ethnic, multicultural, and religiously differentiated population that streamed into the area following the discovery of gold created a colorful but socially tense situation. Each ethnic group was torn between maintaining traditions unique to the home culture while, for the sake of survival, trying to integrate into the diverse, cosmopolitan atmosphere of the Bay Area culture. This kind of disruption of cultural worldviews creates a sociological situation which is ripe for the recruitment of the lost, alone, and alienated into new religious movements that provide an "interior map" to guide the seeker toward the source of strong identity and self-worth. San Francisco really developed as a city of immigrants. By 1880, 60 percent of its population was either foreign-born or children of foreign-born parents. Relationships between different immigrant groups played a major role in every level of the city's growth: politics, economics, culture, and, of course, religion.

Regardless of its unsteady economic and social conditions, Northern Californians were concerned with culture, especially education. Theirs was an open, tolerant, vibrant experimental culture that lent itself to spiritual questioning and the study and discussion of religious perspectives. Members of the intelligentsia, such as Joseph Le Conte, a leading philosopher and scientist at the University of California, or Thomas Starr King, an influential theologian, espoused a progressive, rational, reforming philosophy of life that reverberated with the metaphysician's emphasis on Mind and its powers. Le Conte, in fact, taught a version of evolutionary theism and related his inner musings to the physical Californian environment; because of its spaciousness and grandeur, its healthfulness and abundant natural wonders, California offered a special opportunity for humankind to fuse ethics and science. The combination of a rational, mental approach to life's problems coupled with a free-wheeling cultural environment provided a fertile field for the growth of metaphysical religion.

Unlike Northern California, Los Angeles and the southern region was not settled by young, idealistic risk-takers or predominantly first-generation immigrants from other lands. Southern California was settled by relatively affluent, enculturated, financially secure Protestant Americans with marketable skills, born, for the most part, in the Midwest. They came from Illinois, Indiana, Ohio, Missouri to escape the drudgery of their lives and to create pristine Protestant communities in the ideal Californian climate. It is important to point out that the good life and personal fulfillment were never expressed socially in what might be described as a "Northern California bohemian" manner. The immigrants to Southern California were religious, and they were reformers. Many communities, such as Compton, Westminster, even Hollywood, were begun as ideal communities centering around a specific Protestant denomination. And while many settlers left behind their ties to more traditional religious organizations, the cultural ambience was, nevertheless, permeated with traditional Midwestern values: moral purity, the sanctity of the home, social justice, and the purification of the social order.

The Christian Science and New Thought worldview, with its emphasis on order, mental clarity, and perfection, could be quite appealing to a Southern California citizen, particularly one who was straining at the bit against the more restrictive theological concepts in traditional Protestant Christianity. But two other factors conspired to make metaphysics highly popular in the Southland. First, was the aforementioned "health rush" that took the southern region by storm in the late 1900s. The mystique of the Southern California healing potential drew thousands of invalids, or would-be invalids, to Los Angeles. One observer, Mark Lee Luther, offers this colorful description of health seekers in Los Angeles:

. . . a vast amount of therapeutic lore was to be had for nothing in Westlake Park. The elderly men and women, hailing chiefly from the Mississippi watershed, who made this pleasance their daily rendezvous, were walking encyclopedias of medical knowledge. They seemed to have experienced all ailments, tried all cures. Allopathy, homeopathy, osteopathy, chiropractic, faith-healing and Christian Science, vegetarianism and unfried food, the bacillus bulgaricus, and the internal bath had each its disciples and propagandists (in McWilliams, 1983, pp. 257-258).

A second factor that contributed to the rise of the metaphysical, mental perspective might best be described as "the insidious attack of lotus-land disease." Even those Midwestern immigrants with the best of intentions found themselves, in time, succumbing to a certain placidity and a tendency toward idleness. Perhaps they found the beautiful, unchanging warmth and sunshine disorienting and the call to leisure disconcerting. Nevertheless, the crisis was recognized and a call went out for methods to regain and maintain the industriousness and competitive edge recollected from a previous existence in cultures to the east. Again, the sober, mental clarity, practical application, and focus on demonstrating abundance present in the metaphysical view offered a strong lifeline to pull those who were intoxicated by the sunny clime out of their idle reveries. In any event, the cultural differences between north and south in no way affected the expansion of Christian Science and New Thought in California.

From the beginning of the emergence of organized metaphysical church bodies—specifically the Church of Christ, Scientist—Californians were ready to catch the fever. Mary Baker Eddy despaired of the "babel in California" and complained that her teachings were being perverted by the more wide-ranging New Thought prophets. As early as 1883, Miranda Rice, a former student of Mrs. Eddy's, had moved to San Francisco and established an office as a practitioner (mental healer). She is probably the unnamed source for Malinda Cramer's healing a few years later. Cramer would become one of the co-founders of a major New Thought movement, Divine Science, but, in 1888, much to Mrs. Eddy's chagrin, she established a "Christian Science Home" at 324 Seventeenth St., San Francisco, and a periodical, *Harmony*, in which she essentially "borrowed" and espoused Mrs. Eddy's metaphysical worldview.

Another student of Mrs. Eddy's, Joseph Adams, wrote to her, in 1886, that the situation in San Francisco was clearly getting out of hand.

Institutes of Metaphysical Science have been started which include the teaching of mind-cure, animal magnetism, mesmerism, spiritualism, clairvoyance, and mediumship; while we, as Christian Scientists, are denounced for having our jacket too straight ("The Christian Scientist Association," *Christian Science Journal* V; Nov. 1887, p. 236).

Again, a key difference arises between New Thought and Mrs. Eddy's expression of "Christian Science." Mrs. Eddy's insistence that her teaching constituted a final revelation precluded any experimentation with divergent mind-cure practices. From the above quote, it is apparent that Eddy Christian Scientists adapted to this type of authoritarianism and, thus, from the more open-ended New Thought perspective, could be accused of "having our jacket too straight." In 1891, Mrs. Eddy would successfully claim the appellation "Christian Science" in a lawsuit which, at least, prevented other metaphysically-minded aspirants from using that name for their practices.

Apparently, three years after his note to Mrs. Eddy, Mr. Adams found a looser jacket. Typical of the defection of talented individuals from Mrs. Eddy's authoritarian movement, Adams launched his own successful career as a New Thought healer, lecturer, and writer. With the news that Emma Curtis Hopkins was planning a teaching/lecture tour in California in 1887, Mrs. Eddy was so concerned that she quickly commissioned a loyal San Jose student, Sue Ella Bradshaw, to move to San Francisco in order to establish a branch church and healing practice.

In Southern California, the first known Christian Science church was founded at Riverside in 1887 by Emma S. Davis, a recently settled Christian Science practitioner. Eighteen ninety-three marked the establishment of the first church in Los Angeles proper, and by the first decade of the twentieth century, it was clear the Christian Science was a viable resource for health seekers in the region. The Christian Science organization does not keep membership figures, but one way to estimate the success of Mrs. Eddy's revelation in the Southland, as well as the entire state, is to peruse the listing of churches, societies, and the names and addresses of practitioners in the *Christian Science Journal*.

According to organizational bylaws, each church must have at least sixteen members, and, since practitioners must make their living solely from their healing work, a logical deduction would equate a healthy flock of practitioners in a given region with a vibrant, expanding Christian Science organization. The 1910-11 Los Angeles telephone directory lists over 100 practitioners! Statewide, in the years 1906-1926, the number of churches rose from 35 to 235, a gain of more than 600 percent. Of course, we have to take into account that the general population was expanding dramatically, but by the mid-century, over 349 churches could be counted in the *Journal* listings. These were the peak years for the Christian Science movement, in California as well as America. In the conclusion to this chapter, we will explore some reasons why Christian Science and most of the other nineteenth-century metaphysical religions have endured a sad—in some cases, virtually a terminal—turn-around in membership. But first, let's return to the early years of the movement and meet other key prophets in the New Thought world.

We left Mary Baker Eddy in a snit over Emma Curtis Hopkins' planned lecture tour of California; and the authoritarian leader had every reason for concern. After her excommunication from the Christian Science organization for theological and economic differences, Hopkins went on to influence every major New Thought figure, including all the key metaphysicians on the California scene: Malinda Cramer of Divine Science, Annie Rix Militz of The Home of Truth, Ernest Holmes of Religious Science, and Myrtle and Charles Fillmore of Unity School of Christianity. A genuine mystic and charismatic lecturer, she would, however, never establish a religious organization of her own. Perhaps it was due to her negative experience in the tightly-run Christian Science movement. In any event, at the time of her death in the 1920s, it was estimated that she had ignited the metaphysical spark in over 50,000 students.

The first New Thought organization in California was probably started by Malinda E. Cramer and was the prototype for the group we know today as Divine Science. After studying with Hopkins, Cramer began a successful healing practice in San Jose. By 1887, she expanded her enterprise by moving to San Francisco and founding the first California-based metaphysical journal, *Harmony*. In addition, she established a San Francisco study center which she called the Home College of Divine Science. In 1889, Cramer moved to Colorado where she joined forces with Althea Brooks Small, Fannie Brooks James, and Nona L. Brooks. The Brooks sisters, who were healed spiritually after studying with one Mrs. McKoy, a student of Hopkins, found themselves in total agreement with Cramer's teachings, and the four women officially founded Divine

Science. This organization functioned with two centers, one in California, one in Denver, until Malinda Cramer died in 1907. Thereafter, the Denver church became the center for study, prayer, and the ordination of ministers and continues in this role to this day.

Of the many institutional strands in the New Thought movement, only two can be identified as "made-in-California" religious organizations. The earliest was The Home of Truth, founded by Annie Rix Militz and her sister Harriet Rix shortly after attending Hopkins' 1887 lecture in San Francisco. The humble beginnings of this organization which would, by the 1920s, have churches all over the West Coast and beyond, started in a small bookshop in San Francisco, known amongst spiritual seekers as "The Pacific Coast Metaphysical Company." Apparently the bookshop served as a mail order source for esoteric books on a wide range of occult, mystical, metaphysical and Eastern religion topics. Before passing these books on to their owners, Militz had a chance to steep herself in the multitudinous expressions of popular religion that titillated the souls of upwardly mobile San Franciscans, an experience that no doubt led her to a basic stance of theological freedom. By 1888, she was teaching Hopkins' metaphysics, and demand for class space was such that the first "Christian Science Home" was established at 420 Turk St. where 150 students could be accommodated at at time. Since the label "Christian Science" was rapidly becoming more of a liability than a positive appellation due to both the negative publicity surrounding Mary Baker Eddy's quest for power and her legal commandeering of the term, Militz soon changed the name of the Turk St. center to Home of Truth.

By the turn of the century, Militz had established Homes of Truth in San Francisco, Alameda, San Diego, Oakland, and San Jose, but it was in Los Angeles that her movement had the greatest success. Hers was the perfect match between organizational dynamics of the movement and sociocultural environment. As we have observed, Los Angeles was settled by conservative Midwesterners who created distinct, pristine communities throughout the expansive Los Angeles basin. Into this idyllic American-suburban-dreamscape comes Annie Rix Militz and the Home of Truth concept. What could better fit scattered yet perfectly maintained communities than a do-it-yourself church built on the theme of "Home?" Militz supplied the "how to" in weekly devotional services published in her periodical, *Master Mind*, and those interested in this type of religious expression provided the "where"—their own homes. An added advantage for the spread of the movement was the advent of electric railways which connected the various pristine communities and offered adherents easy access to important lectures and materials held in Militz's college in downtown Los Angeles, The University of Christ.

Militz also had an important, but largely unacknowledged, influence on the largest New Thought organization, Charles Fillmore's Unity School of Christianity. One of the major difficulties in obtaining an accurate picture of the history of New Thought movements is the tendency for the groups to either take a completely ahistorical stance—of what difference is human history since creation is perfect and complete—or else adhere to an "in house" story that promotes the particular leaders of the organizations as key figures possessed of unparalleled spiritual acumen who arrived at their metaphysical perceptions unassisted by others in the broader New Thought movement. This is certainly the case with Charles Fillmore and the beginnings of the Unity School of Christianity, a major American New Thought organization with headquarters in the Kansas City area.

Official biographers of Fillmore and the movement make little mention of his interest in Christian Science as taught by Eddy and Hopkins and make no mention of Militz' contribution during the formation years of the movement. This in spite of the fact that for years Militz' Bible lessons were the major articles in *Unity* magazine and offered the more wide-ranging Fillmore a theological anchor.

Fillmore himself, however, openly acknowledged his appreciation of Militz as a writer, teacher, and healer, and she even taught the coveted monthly class at Unity headquarters in Kansas City in October of 1900. In a way, Militz sacrificed herself for the Unity movement by providing a forum for Unity ideas in her own periodical and, given her open-minded style, allowing Unity organizations to take over Homes of Truth. In fact, the only remaining Home of Truth—in Alameda—is run by a minister trained in the Unity organization. Interestingly enough, Militz became convinced in her later years that, like Jesus, she would overcome death. Thus, she left no organizational guidance for her church should she depart this realm of consciousness. After her death in 1924 in Los Angeles, Homes of Truth suffered a rapid decline and, as mentioned, only one can still be identified today.

The other "made-in-California" New Thought movement to emerge was Ernest Holmes' United Church of Religious Science, headquartered in Los Angeles. Born in Maine in 1887, around the time Emma Curtis Hopkins was lecturing in San Francisco and Militz was beginning her ministry, this "Johnny-come-lately" to the New Thought world nevertheless built a religious organization second only to Unity in numbers of adherents. As a young man, Holmes absorbed writings by Emerson, Eddy, Evans, and other prominent metaphysicians and eventually was ordained a Divine Science minister. His career was launched, in 1916, after a public lecture in the Los Angeles metaphysical library on the "fundamentals" that could be found in all New Thought philosophies.

Holmes possessed characteristics that made him a natural religious leader. He was a charismatic speaker who could also write with clarity and a kind of subdued passion so attractive to the metaphysical crowd. In fact his textbook, *Science of Mind*, first published in 1926, has become a classic in American religious literature.

During the years 1916-1920, Holmes traveled the nation stirring crowds in major cities such as New York and Philadelphia. His first major writings, *Creative Mind* (1918) and *Creative Mind and Success* (1919), were widely read and established him as a leader in the New Thought field. He even studied mysticism with the aging Emma Curtis Hopkins in New York City before returning to Los Angeles to institutionalize his worldview. Drawing on the institutional genius of Mary Baker Eddy, Holmes incorporated the Institute of Religious Science and School of Philosophy which, in 1935, moved to its present home at 3251 West Sixth Street in Los Angeles.

Until his death in 1960, Holmes led something of a charmed life in Los Angeles as Religious Science grew to be the second largest New Thought group in America. He escaped the type of public animosity that tormented earlier metaphysicians, and, due in part to his wife's social connections, Holmes led an almost regal life, respected by academicians in the Philosophy Department at the University of Southern California and fawned over by the spiritually searching Hollywood crowd. To this day, the metaphysical library housed in the church's headquarters is one of the best in the nation.

Christian Science and New Thought in the Later Twentieth Century

In 1980, the International New Thought Alliance, the governing body of the variegated groups, listed eighty-seven centers in California making the "Golden State" by far the most active metaphysical center. But the situation is not all sunshine in California or, for that matter, the nation in terms of the ability of these groups to grow into the twenty-first century. Unlike the California Mormons, who are developing a model for the globalization of that religion in the twenty-first century, California metaphysicians are faced with a dilemma: adapt or die as religious alternatives. The change that is needed tends to be one of style rather than ritual practices or basic philosophy.

For instance, as one wag historian has put it, the advent of penicillin marked the inevitable decline of the mind-cure movement. To be sure, improvements in health care within the medical profession since the nineteenth century have been dramatic. Whereas a nineteenth-century invalid probably had just as good a chance of survival in the hands of a Christian Science practitioner as those of a medical doctor, today members of the American Medical Association have a hegemonic grasp on the health field. To put it simply, Americans, for the most part, feel comfortable trusting their bodies to a secular healing profession while leaving the maintenance of their souls to members of the clergy. Recently, the Christian Science movement has been ridden with turmoil given the manslaughter convictions of parents whose children died of rather common ailments in the hands of a Christian Science practitioner. Where once Christian Scientists had the power to fend off secular attacks on their unique healing perspective, winds of change blow cold on religious freedom that snuffs out the lives of defenseless children.

On the other hand, nationwide there has been an increase in holistic healing practices that span the field from ancient pagan or Native American rituals, ointments, and cures to positive thinking, meditative practices, crystal work, Tarot, macrobiotic diet, and a variety of other healing methods loosely aligned with "New Age" metaphysics. What we are seeing in California—and, as always, California acts as a cultural microcosm for the greater nation—is a trend in the more successful metaphysical churches to accommodate their teachings to include the more eclectic New Age themes.

Of course, for Christian Science churches this is institutionally impossible, and, unless they can break out of the ironclad liturgical pattern delineated by Mrs. Eddy one hundred years ago, they will fail. A visit to even the most successful Christian Science church in Los Angeles or San Jose or San Francisco reveals pews peopled by gray, blue, or bald-headed believers. The church is just not attracting the next generation.

Within the New Thought churches, the pattern of success is less institutionally defined but arises in the context of individual churches with leaders who sense the need for adaptation, and implement it in one form or another. For instance, while the main Religious Science complex in downtown Los Angeles struggles to fend off bankruptcy, just down the freeway in Huntington Beach the Religious Science church is extremely successful under the leadership of a young, charismatic healer whose ministry reverberates with Shirley MacLaine's brand of New Age enthusiasm. The Unity Church in Santa Barbara gains new adherents by offering "channeling" sessions during the week. The last Home of Truth in Alameda survives because the Unity-trained ministers use lively music and crystal work to complement their basic metaphysical teachings.

A final challenge to the continued growth of our nineteenth-century metaphysical movements is the ironic fact that the essence of their teaching has been co-opted by leaders in mainstream Protestant churches and by American culture itself. Preachers such as California's Robert Schuller or his predecessor, New York's Norman Vincent Peale, have taken the "positive thinking" message of New Thought and adapted it to a quasi-orthodox Protestant Christian theological stance. Protestant, Catholic, and Jewish religious writers have produced books that top the sales charts while offering thinly disguised New Thought ideas. The most popular title, Norman Vincent Peale's *The Power of Positive Thinking*, sold two million copies! Others include Bishop Fulton Sheen's *Peace of Soul* and Rabbi Joshua Liebman's *Peace of Mind*.

An article in the *New York Times* (September 29, 1986) noted that New Thought principles, now called New Age, permeate American society. For example, commercial slogans such as "Be all you can be" (U.S. Armed Forces), "Master the possibilities" (MasterCard), or "To know no boundaries" (Merrill Lynch) suggest that human beings have the capacity to create their own realities through control of mental attitude.

There has always been a kind of "frontier desire" on the part of Americans, a quest to push back boundaries, overcome limitations, and ascend above the commonplace in order to attain the substance of dreams. While the religious institutions that represent nineteenth-century metaphysical sectarianism may go the way of the dinosaur, it was the California experience that allowed these movements to eventually have this kind of "perfection in paradise" impact on the broader American society.

SOURCES AND FURTHER READING

Ahlstrom, Sydney E. *A Religious History of the American People.* Garden City, NY: Doubleday and Co., 1975. 2 Vols.
Braden, Charles S. *Christian Science Today: Power, Policy, Practice.* Dallas: SMU Press, 1989.
—. *Spirits in Rebellion.* (Dallas: SMU Press). 1963.
Gottschalk, Stephen. *The Emergence of Christian Science in American Religious Life.* Berkeley: University of California Press, 1973.
Judah, J. Stillson. *The History and Philosophy of the Metaphysical Movements in America.* Philadelphia: Westminster Pres,. 1967.
McLoughlin, William G. *Revivals, Awakenings, and Reform.* Chicago: University of Chicago, 1978.
McWilliams, Carey. *Southern California: An Island on the Land.* Salt Lake City: Peregrine Books, 1983.
Melton, J. Gordon. *The Encyclopedia of American Religions.* Detroit: Gale Research Co., 1988.
Simmons, John K. *The Ascension of Annie Rix Militz and the Home(s) of Truth: Perfection Meets Paradise in Early Twentieth Century Los Angeles* (unpublished dissertation), 1987.

6 Cultivating Spirits in California: Thomas Lake Harris and Christian Spiritualism

If on a summer's day in the 1870s you happened to travel a ways north of Santa Rosa in the Sonoma Valley, you might have come across a small farm-cum-winery called Fountain Grove. Out in the vineyards the English author and one-time member of Parliament, Laurence Oliphant, might have been seen patiently pulling weeds along with a small army of other men, all under the direction of a one-time samurai, Kanaye Nagasawa. In the kitchen of the small Victorian farmhouse that stood at the center of Fountain Grove, you would probably have encountered Laurence's mother, Lady Maria Oliphant, quietly doing the dishes, while in the parlor, California's poet-laureate Edwin Markham listened in rapt attention as the mysterious master of Fountain Grove extemporized in polished verse about his latest communication with the dead.

Who was this strange man in the heavy frock coat, slowly pacing the small study and reciting quatrain after endless quatrain in a low, grave voice? Who was this man who commanded the allegiance of wealthy English and Japanese aristocrats, and by dint of whose charisma they had given up the luxuries of life to till the soil on the outskirts of an obscure and isolated California town? Thomas Lake Harris was no ordinary California farmer: visionary, mystic, and seer, Harris was a genuine American prophet who, by communing with spirits of the dead, came to conceive a radically new interpretation of the Christian mystery. Harris' synthesis of

Spiritualism and Christianity represented one of the most fascinating new sects nineteenth-century California had ever seen.

If the truth be told, however, Harris' movement was perhaps the least influential and shortest lived of all the sectarian movements we have been studying. And yet Christian spiritualism as a whole represents such an interesting and eclectic blend of nineteenth-century American religious resources that it cannot be passed over in silence. Like Christian Science and New Thought, Christian Spiritualism took its cues from the teachings of Emanuel Swedenborg and the "scientific" hypotheses of Anton Mesmer, and yet, unlike these other, successful sects, Christian Spiritualism did not survive into the twentieth century. The question to be addressed in this chapter is why. Focusing on California's Harris and his Fountain Grove movement, we will suggest possible reasons for the sudden blossoming and precipitous fade of Christian Spiritualism in the United States and California.

First, however, it will be useful to review the history of Spiritualism and to underscore how important the phenomenon once was in the United States. In the introduction to this volume we spoke in passing about something scholars have come to call worldviews. Worldviews form a comprehensive perspective on the structure and function of the universe and thus allow individuals to discover their place in this structure and the rules by which they are to live their lives in it. Sociologists have claimed that beyond individual orientation, a shared worldview is characteristic of any unified society, while competing worldviews lead to the fracturing of the social order. Everyone seems at least intuitively aware of this, as can be witnessed by the ferocious, sometimes mindless tenacity with which people fight to maintain their shared worldview.

For early men and women worldviews had been provided by means of revelation, that is, the non-rational perception of totalizing divine knowledge usually articulated in the form of myth or in prescriptive law. First transmitted orally, this knowledge was later recorded in written form and organized into scripture. In the West, the most important examples of this have been the Hebrew and Christian Bibles. Judaism and Christianity, however, are only two such religions organized around such revelation.

Beginning in the European Renaissance (fourteenth–sixteenth centuries) and culminating during the period called the Enlightenment (seventeenth–eighteenth centuries), the authority of the

Christian revelation came to be seriously challenged. By combining reason with empirical observation, it came to be believed that true knowledge could only be that which proceeded from the senses, and that the correct interpretation of such knowledge could only be confirmed inductively by what came to be called the scientific method. Since the Christian revelation, arriving as it did through extrasensory channels, could therefore no longer be trusted, the Christian worldview that had been elaborated from it was called into question too.

Of course, this did not mean that the ancient Judeo-Christian worldview was summarily abandoned. The majority of people continued to fervently believe in the truth of their received myths. Many—while fully expecting science to provide a new and more truthful worldview in the future—also saw that the rejection of the Judeo-Christian worldview would have entailed grave structural problems for society at large and perceived the efficacy in maintaining tradition. Still others sought to adapt the Judeo-Christian tradition to the demands of science, developing what would become Deism, a faith in which many of the old features and myths, such as a unique creator God, were retained and yet modified so as to be more "scientifically rational."

In America, Deism and Enlightenment rationalism were very influential in initiating the United States' political institutions, as well as essaying a new national identity. A fervent belief in the efficacy of science for the improvement of man became widespread, especially in the beginning of America's industrialization in the early nineteenth century. Nevertheless, the United States was a country firmly rooted in its Protestant past, and, as the persistence of Protestant Christianity until the present day demonstrates, many were not eager to give up their Christian past just because it clashed with the exigencies of the present. Some Christians dealt with the pressure of rationalization by reaffirming their faith through more liberal and less literalistic interpretations of the Christian myths. Still others reaffirmed their faith by claiming new revelations which either corroborated or corrected the interpretations of the old ones. So widespread did this last phenomena become in the United States that the receiving of "new light" has come to be seen as one of the four defining characteristics of American religion. In its American guise it is called Illuminism, and we have already encountered it in Mormonism, Adventism and in Christian Science.

In this chapter we will be dealing with Spiritualism, a particular type of American Illuminism which arose and flourished for a time both in the United States and, in a particularly interesting form, in California. Spiritualism is the belief that the dead continue to exist in some shadowy, non-physical intermediary world beyond this one, and that through psychic means—ESP, mediumship, etc.—these dead can communicate their secrets to the living. Such communication was thought to be scientifically verifiable and rationally explainable. Now, while Spiritualism as it arose in the United States was an overwhelmingly secular phenomena, Christian Spiritualism is interesting and important in the light of the foregoing discussion because it was a concerted effort to verify (and many times "correct") the Christian revelation from a (supposedly) scientifically verifiable source: the spirits of the familiar dead.

In the West, Spiritualism in any form remained proscribed and was not openly practiced until the European Enlightenment of the eighteenth century. Two factors influenced its sudden rise. First, in an increasingly rational universe, occult phenomena such as communication with spirits no longer posed much of a threat to the existing Christian order. The Enlightenment itself, having called into question the very idea of the immortality of the soul, made many scorn the very notion of spirit communication as mere superstition. This, however, gave others who did indeed accept spirit communication as a genuine phenomenon a new-found freedom to explore it—and explore it they did.

Perhaps paradoxically, some saw Spiritualism as the only scientific way of proving the existence of the immortality of the soul and corroborating the truths taught by Christianity. Many pietists of the period, Wesleyans and Methodists for example, were especially interested in this enterprise. The major problem, however, was that what the spirits were reported to have said did not always correspond with received dogma. Thus, naturally enough in this era of relative religious freedom, new religious syntheses arose which attempted to reconcile the new spirit revelations with traditional Christian dogma.

Probably the most important and influential of these new sectarian syntheses resulted in the faith known as Swedenborgianism. We have already mentioned the name of Swedenborg in connection with the rise of Christian Science and New Thought in the last chapter. Here, it will be valuable to go into a bit more detail about the teachings of this visionary Swede. In the late 1700s Swedenborg claimed to have made contact with spirits and that, in visions, he was allowed to travel to spirit realms whence he received a new revelation about the nature of God, human life, and the survival of the soul after death. In six long books, Swedenborg set forth an elaborate, systematized overview of this new revelation.

The heart of Swedenborg's thought consisted of the "law of correspondences," according to which there are two levels of created existence, the physical and the spiritual. Tying these two worlds together are their exact, one-to-one correspondences. When a person dies, he or she passes on to a world substantially like this one, except for the fact there is no bodily resurrection: men and women exist as discarnate spirits.

The composition of the spirit world is complex: according to Swedenborg there are six spiritual spheres beyond the material world, three belonging to heaven and three belonging to hell. Immediately upon death, a person passes to the lowest level of either heaven or hell—lowest in terms of closeness to earth. Thus, from these lower levels contact between spirits and man is still possible, as is communication of the supernatural truths newly acquired by the recently departed. Despite his elaborate cosmology, Swedenborg was still a believing Christian and felt that nothing in his new revelation was inconsistent with Christian dogma. He wrote long commentaries detailing the spiritual meaning of Christian scripture and felt his work both complemented and completed the Christian worldview.

Ignored in his own country, Swedenborg's ideas found sympathetic ears in England. Shortly after the seer's death in 1772, a church based on his promise was formed in London. From there members of this new "Swedenborgian" faith immigrated to America where they founded a Swedenborg society in Baltimore in 1792. One of the most famous early propagators of Swedenborgianism in America was John Chapman (1774-1847). Also known as "Johnny Appleseed," Chapman planted apple seeds and distributed Swedenborgian literature while traveling through the Ohio Valley.

Although Swedenborgianism had existed in the United States for decades, in was not until the late 1840s that the general concept of Spiritualism really captured the American imagination. On March 31, 1848 Kate Fox came to realize that the strange rapping noises frequently heard in her home in Hydesville, New York, were actually a form of spirit communication. By developing a system of claps and raps, Kate and her sisters began to communicate on a regular basis with this spirit who, it was claimed, was that of a man murdered there years before. The newspapers of the day gave this story wide play, and from then on the Spiritualist medium would become a fixture in American society for the rest of the century.

For the most part, Spiritualist mediums were motivated by commercial interests (mediumship was one of the few high-paying vocations for women in the nineteenth century), and the public that patronized them were more interested in novelty or the communication with loved ones than they were in obtaining spiritual insights. There were others, however—a rather small minority—who, like Swedenborg before them, saw in mediumship a source of revelation and set about to act on this new revelation. Part of the appeal of Spiritualism for these religious seekers was that, unlike previous revelation, the phenomenon of mediumship was repeatable and hence susceptible to scientific investigation. For two of the most successful creators of nineteenth-century spiritualist sectarian movements—Andrew Jackson Davis and Thomas Lake Harris—the original appeal of Spiritualism was exactly its supposed scientific rationality.

Andrew Jackson Davis (1826-1910), the father of the first coherent American worldview based on Spiritualism, came to the practice by way of Mesmerism. Introduced from France to the United States in 1832, Mesmerism was an elaborate, pseudoscientific explanation of the phenomenon today called hypnotism which posited the magnetic transference of an invisible fluid as the means by which the hypnotist acted on his subject. Davis, intrigued by this explanation of hypnotism, became even more interested when he found that he was uniquely susceptible to the hypnotic state himself, and that while in this state he could accurately diagnose illness. Even more exciting, however, Davis also found that his hypnotic states were akin to mediumistic trances, and, indeed, Davis came to claim spirit contacts. As different as the two phenomena of Mesmerism and Spiritualism may seem, the two practices were often linked in the popular mind familiar with such things, since the invisible "magnetic" fluid was thought not only to psychically connect living human beings to each other, but also the living to the dead.

While living in Poughkeepsie, New York, during the decade of the 1840s, Davis taught himself reliable methods of auto-hypnotism, and he came to claim contact with a number of very famous spirits. Galen, the ancient Greek physician, was a frequent interlocutor, as was Emanuel Swedenborg himself. Although primarily gaining fame as a psychic healer, Davis soon became a prolific and popular writer of Spiritualist tracts. Echoing elements of Swedenborgianism, Davis synthesized a metaphysical system with a peculiarly American spin: instead of Swedenborg's six worlds, Davis extended his cosmology infinitely. According to Davis the earth was indeed surrounded by six spheres, each representing higher and more perfect realms of spiritual existence. After death, the soul progressed through these six planes on its way to God. This, however, was an endless process of growth, for once the sixth plane had been reached, another six appeared, and so on through eternity.

Davis originally attempted to incorporate Christianity into his Spiritualism, but he later came to reject it as too constrictingly dogmatic. The Spiritualist movement which subsequently grew from Davis' teachings thus remained largely ambivalent toward the Christian faith. The majority of serious Spiritualists were, for the most part, marked by extremely independent and non-dogmatic frames of mind; after all, with Spiritualism, potentially anyone could become a prophet. For this reason, "the Spiritualist movement," such as it was, was bound together by the single tenet of spirit communication and always tolerated a wide variety of theological opinion, Christian or otherwise. It was partly due to this fact that the "Davisian" Spiritualist movement never gained the cohesion it needed to become a true sect.

Despite this last fact, mainline Protestantism nevertheless actively agitated against Spiritualism of any kind during the period from 1850 to 1870. The liberalizing influences of the Enlightenment notwithstanding, some still felt that Spiritualism was the work of the devil; others felt that it tended to undermine the authority of scripture and reinforced contemporary currents of religious liberalism and theological rationalism as represented by Unitarianism and Universalism. Nevertheless, in the face of this hostility from the Protestant mainstream—or perhaps because of it—Davis' teachings spread far and wide across the nation. Even on the far shores of California the writings of the "Poughkeepsie seer" could be found in some of the more eclectic bookstores of San Francisco.

Spiritualism and California

Spiritualism in the form of the traveling medium had appeared in California before the Civil War, but it was only after the conclusion of that war that an indigenous Spiritualist movement a la Davis arose. By 1867, Spiritualists in Northern California were printing their own paper, *The Banner of Progress*. It ran for two years. Later, in 1880, another Spiritualist newspaper appeared called *Light for All*. It lasted a year.

Although relatively few in number, California sectarian Spiritualists still did not escape the attacks of the mainline Protestant denominations. Spiritualist teachings on revelation, cosmology and life after death were just as radical in California as they were in other parts of the Union. Nevertheless, as we have mentioned before, California during these formative years had a transient, cosmopolitan and, for the most part, unchurched population which valued its independence and was more concerned with the acquisition of wealth and physical comfort than it was in spiritual values. An anarchic tolerance developed in this environment which, while not especially congenial to Spiritualism, was not especially hostile to it either.

It was into this environment that Thomas Lake Harris (1823-1906) brought his Christian Spiritualist community in 1875. Harris claimed that his spirit guides had led him to the Pacific shores of California, there to await new revelations and, ultimately, the end of the world. The prophet had already started two semi-socialistic communities in the East, but, by 1881, he had moved all his members to a 1,400-acre estate near Santa Rosa, which he christened Fountain Grove.

Harris was born in England in 1823 and emigrated with his parents to New York state five years later. Chafing under his strict Calvinist upbringing, Harris became a theological liberal as a teenager and a Universalist minister at age twenty. Increasingly, however, Harris came to reject Universalism because of what he considered the narrowness of its dogma and—mirroring the perfectionism of the day—its lack of social conscience. Harris soon found himself attracted to the Spiritualism of Andrew Jackson Davis, eventually becoming one of the seer's most devoted disciples—so devoted in fact, that he resigned his Universalist post in 1847 and became a full-time popular lecturer on Davis' theories. Although the association with the Poughkeepsie seer was quickly broken (Harris apparently objected to Davis's relaxed attitudes toward sex), Harris did come in contact with the teachings of Swedenborg through Davis. Despite his youthful rejection of Calvinism, Harris by this time had returned to embrace the literal truths of the Christian myth and found in Swedenborgianism a Christian Spiritualist synthesis which could accommodate these truths. Part of Harris' new-found literalism included his acceptance of a heaven and hell (both ideas rejected by both Universalism and by Davis' pantheism), and—common for his time as we have seen— an increasing obsession with Adventism.

Harris was also deeply impressed by the vision for rejuvenated mankind and a prescription for communal living offered by Swedenborg. After serving for some time as pastor to a Swedenborgian congregation in New York City, Harris and another Christian Spiritualist, J. L. Scott, co-founded a cooperative agricultural community in Mountain Cove, West Virginia in 1851. Both Harris and Scott claimed to be perfect mediums through which the divine instructions for the operation of the colony would be received. Mountain Cove ultimately failed, perhaps because, as it was rumored, Harris and Scott failed to correctly predict the date of the Advent; in any case, Harris reluctantly returned to his New York congregation. Nevertheless, the Mountain Cove experiment confirmed Harris in his passion to found a Christian Spiritualist community devoted to harmonious communal living, oriented toward the Advent, and directed by his exclusive mediumship. It seems that along with Harris's Illuminism, Millennialism and Perfectionism, Universalism did not have a place.

The fruits of Harris's mediumship had been maturing throughout the decade of the 1850s. Harris wrote tirelessly, pouring out his communications in books of poetry, prose and in the newly-founded journal, *The Herald of the Light*, much of which he wrote himself. Increasingly, Harris's ideas deviated from Swedenborg's, and, in 1857, Harris proclaimed to his parishioners that he had received a new revelation from a group of spiritual worthies. The spirit of Swedenborg himself had appointed Harris the new messenger of God. His congregation was appalled, and Harris was summarily dismissed. Far from daunted, however, Harris, in classical sectarian manner, proclaimed himself a scorned prophet, and set about to create a new church which would enshrine his own new Christian Spiritualist promise and plan.

The Theology of the Divine Breath

Harris claimed that through his spiritual guides he, like Swedenborg, had been privileged to know the true—Spiritualist—meaning of scripture. According to Harris, this spiritual reading revealed to him two fundamental things: first, it documented the true history of the world and allowed him thus to anticipate the exact date of its end; and secondly, it revealed a manner in which man could reach spiritual perfection in this life, perfection which would allow a small group to survive the tribulations of the apocalypse to form the remnant millennial kingdom.

In Harris' cosmology, three levels of existence were posited: the material, the spiritual, and the celestial or divine. Between levels of creation there was a strict correspondence maintained by the flow of God's Divine Breath (the Holy Spirit) between them. By opening one's "spiritual lungs" to this breath, one could participate in this life in the higher realms and thus experience "regeneration" or purification, not to mention communication with higher spirits. It was just such divine breathing that the elect would have to master to deserve God's coming kingdom.

According to Harris' spiritual reading of the Old and New Testaments, Adam and Eve had lived in a golden age in which they freely inhaled the Holy Spirit. With the Fall, however, mankind had lost most of the powers of this divine respiration. Jesus' mission therefore included bringing back the secret of this respiration. Unfortunately, Jesus' Apostles were deemed unfit to propagate it since, according to Harris, they were corrupted by the desire for worldly power. For this reason Jesus had proclaimed his Second Coming, a time in which the secret of respiration would again be reintroduced into the world by a "pivotal man" who would have the power and the permission to teach this secret to a select group. Increasingly, Harris came to see himself in this role.

Traveling to England and Scotland in 1859, Harris gathered around him a group of followers who, impressed by his Spiritualist promise and plan, formed the Brotherhood of the New Life, an organization dedicated to cultivating the Divine Breath in a communal setting. By dint of his charismatic personality Harris was able to attract followers—notably the wealthy Laurence Oliphant and his mother, Lady Oliphant—both of whom shared his dream of an earthly utopia and had the skills and the money to finance it. Returning to America, Harris had, by 1868, set up two such communities, one near Wassaic, New York, and the other on the shores of Lake Erie in Brocton. Including the Oliphants, both communities boasted seventy-five members, all of whom, regardless of social station, Harris treated with autocratic rigor. Harris had the gift of being able to attract people from many walks of life, from rural American farmers to Japanese aristocrats, and to inspire in them an almost blind obedience in service to his communities, collectively called "The Use."

Financially the colonies throve, dedicated as they were to small business, animal husbandry and, most importantly, the lucrative pursuit of viticulture. One of the more pragmatic reasons given for the consolidation of the Brotherhood in California was the suitability of the area around Santa Rosa for vineyards and the production of fine wine. Whatever the reasons may have been, the California colony too was initially quite successful, both spiritually and financially—at least during the 1880s. Harris and his community were seen as eccentric, but they paid their bills on time, employed many during the harvests, and produced award-winning wines sold exclusively in their own wine shop in New York City. In the California of the time, this was all that anyone asked. Despite the oddness of some of his doctrines and the secrecy with which he kept his community cloaked, the local business communities feted Harris on occasion, and he was courted by the local Masons. If the mainline Protestant denominations knew of his presence in California—and this is likely—they did nothing to attack him.

Harmony in paradise did not last long, however, as it rarely does. In 1881, Harris' most famous follower, the English aristocrat Oliphant, had claimed that he too had achieved spiritual "respiration," and was in communication with higher spirits. Unfortunately, these new communications contradicted Harris' rule. Oliphant, a brilliant author and one-time member of Parliament, was a charismatic man in his own right, and his pronouncements carried weight with some in the community. A power struggle ensued. Soon, Oliphant, who had sunk thousands of dollars in the Fountain Grove experiment, sued Harris and in time recovered the bulk of his money. Oliphant then moved to Palestine, there purchasing the plains of Armageddon and setting up his own Christian Spiritualist community very much along the lines of the California "Use."

Harris meanwhile never completely recovered from the blow, financially or spiritually; his authority threatened, the prophet became even more autocratic and his rule of the community more erratic.

This indeed illustrates one of the key factors for the lack of success of Spiritualism as a coherent sectarian movement in America. Prophecy in spiritualism depended on mediumship, and mediumship depended for the most part on mastering certain physical laws—laws which were immutable and available to anyone through reason. Essentially, then, one did not have to be chosen by God to be a prophet; the very universality of physical law meant that, potentially, anyone could have access to the secrets of the spiritual world. Personal charisma and a convoluted plan such as Harris' "Twelve Steps to Higher Respiration" were often not enough to prevent those of an individualistic bent from becoming prophets in their own right.

Although Oliphant's challenge did irreversible damage to Harris' prestige, and there are indications that his California community went into a slow decline from that point on, Fountain Grove probably would have lasted some years more if another, more mundane scandal had not soon hastened its demise. Considering Harris' break with Andrew Jackson Davis over Davis' disdain for conventional morality, the immediate cause of this scandal is more than a little ironic. Taking Genesis at its word, Harris conceived of God as bisexual. After all, Harris reasoned, if God created man in his image, "male and female created He them," then it was logical to assume that God contained both sexes. Thus, the god-like free respiration in the spirit could only be obtained when the sexes were united; such sexual union, however, would occur on a spiritual, not an earthly plane. Luckily, every person was associated with a spiritual "counterpart" of the opposite sex who existed on one of the heavenly planes. Union was achieved only through arduously progressing through the twelve step process of Higher Respiration and thus only spiritually advanced beings could experience it: thus, Adam had his Eve, Jesus had his "Yessa," and Harris had his counterpart, the "Lily Queen."

The rigorous process under which Harris' devotees labored in his California colony was therefore essentially an attempt to achieve a "spiritual" sexual union. This, and the fact that Harris tended to describe this process in fairly explicit language, produced over time a backlash of rumor, distortion, and innuendo. Tales of slavery and sexual impropriety—never substantiated, but never refuted—began to filter out of Fountain Grove and were greedily disseminated by the press, ever hungry for a sex scandal. Harris, although morbidly sensitive about his reputation, nevertheless refused to challenge the growing tide of sensational newspaper reports about him and his California colony. In time, local public opinion, which had been indifferent at best, became inflamed with curiosity; the privacy of the California "Use" could no longer be maintained. Vilified in the local press and ceaselessly gawked at by sensation-seeking Santa Rosans, the prophet finally abandoned his California colony for Europe in 1892. Eventually Harris settled in New York and spent his remaining years there ineffectually directing Fountain Grove from afar. Without Harris' charisma, however, the Fountain Grove experiment quickly disintegrated, although the winery continued to produce until Prohibition closed it in 1934. Harris himself "passed to a higher sphere" at the age of eighty-three in 1906.

Although specifically "Christian" Spiritualism can be said to have died in California after the demise of Fountain Grove, the Illuminist promise of Spiritualism has lived on in the hearts of many Californians well into the twentieth century. One author has recently argued that today's "channeling" is a direct descendent of Spiritualist ideas of the nineteenth century. Indeed, the definition given of channeling today—"the communication of information to or through a physically embodied human being from a source that is said to exist on some other level or dimension of reality than the physical as we know it"—sounds suspiciously like the classical definition given for Spiritualism a century before. It is perhaps not surprising then that in California channeling beings from other worlds actually started as early as 1886, when Frederick S. Oliver contacted "Phylos the Tibetan" on the slopes of Mt. Shasta. Nor is it surprising that it is estimated today that the greater Los Angeles area plays host to the greatest density of professional channelers in the world. The majority of these channelers and their followers, however, have an explicitly non-Christian focus. Illuminism in a Christian guise seems not to have survived in California in the highly intellectual environment of the Spiritualist's darkened parlor; rather, in twentieth-century California, it reappears in the highly emotional environment of the Pentacostalist revival hall. It is to Pentecostalism, therefore, that we turn next.

SOURCES AND FURTHER READING

Hine, Robert V. *California's Utopian Colonies*. San Marino, Ca.: The Huntington Library, 1953.

Klimo, Jon. *Channeling: Investigations on Receiving Information from Paranormal Sources*. Los Angeles: Jeremy P. Tarcher, Inc., 1987.

Moore, Laurence R. *In Search of White Crows: Spiritualism, Parapsychology, and American Culture*. New York: Oxford University Press, 1977.

Melton, Gordon J. *The Encyclopedia of American Religions*, 3rd edition. Detroit: Gale Research, 1989.

Schneider, Herbert W., and Lawton, George. *A Prophet and a Pilgrim: Being the Incredible History of Thomas Lake Harris and Laurence Oliphant; Their Sexual Mysticisms and Utopian Communities Amply Documented to Confound the Skeptic*. New York: Columbia University Press, 1942.

7 Pentecostalism in California

The story of the Holiness-Pentecostal movement in the United States reveals a classic paradox in the world of religion and religious movements. The religious impulse propels a believer toward transcendent, extraordinary experience. Yet in the institutionalization of that very experience, the focus of the group can be turned away from spiritual concerns as the congregation, quite understandably, goes about the business of dressing raw religious experience in the trappings of the dominant culture. We are speaking here of the tension between religion and culture. On one hand, religious organizations provide structure; they are launching pads for the experiential journey into the transcendent, the link between form and formlessness, tradition and eternity. On the other hand, as we have already noted in our opening comments on sectarianism, enculturation can smother authentic religious experience. In time, believers may feel compelled to throw off excess institutional baggage in an attempt to renew the true faith. When this occurs, a new sect is born.

The Holiness-Pentecostal movement is a classic example of sectarian behavior and one that reverberates with a recurring theme in American/Californian religious history—the quest for "perfection in paradise." In this chapter, we will track the development of these two interconnected movements, most notably, in the work of Phineas F. Bresee, a charismatic Nazarene minister, and William J.

Seymour who is credited with initiating one of the greatest religious revivals in American history—the Azusa Street revival in Los Angeles. But first it will be helpful for us to review the historical roots of the Holiness movement and those of its lively cousin, Pentecostalism.

A Short History of the Holiness Movement

While the actual Holiness movement emerged during the spiritually frenetic times immediately following the Second Great Awakening, the theological/experiential roots are found in the Methodist movement. John Wesley, founder of Methodism, was struck by Christ's call, "Be ye perfect as my father in heaven is perfect" (Matt. 5:48). For Wesley, the real challenge in Christ's teaching was a distinct call to perfection in this life. As prophet, he articulated a new promise and provided a plan for reaching new levels of Christian perfection. Experientially, a state of holiness, characterized by sinlessness and love, could be attained by Christians through a process called sanctification. The sanctification experience, sometimes called the second blessing or second work of grace, envelops the believer after the experience of being born again (justification) and involves an inward cleansing of sin, the indwelling of the Holy Spirit, and the empowerment of the believer to live a life of perfect holiness.

Of course this variety of "can-do" spirit conflicted with standard Christian teaching on the sinful nature of humankind and the sovereignty of God in guiding human redemption. But as we mentioned in our discussion of the great periods of cultural upheaval called Awakenings, Christians in the early nineteenth century had, for the most part, thrown aside the constricting theological chains familiar to Puritan colonists. Thus, once again, the American experience provided the possibility and the place for innovative prophets with sectarian visions.

While Wesley may be credited with initiating a holiness quest, he certainly had help from the great theologians and evangelists of the First Awakening, in particular, Jonathan Edwards and George Whitefield. These eighteenth-century religious leaders reinterpreted key Protestant concepts like predestination and original sin and, in so doing, put a "made in America" stamp on God's millennial plan. Edwards, in the mid-eighteenth century, did more than any other religious leader to bridge the gap between God and human beings. Like a master psychologist, he assuaged human anxiety over impending salvation, or lack thereof, by not only clarifying the idea of conversion and giving it sound doctrinal standing but also providing a set of clearly defined steps that, once followed, propelled the doubtful believer into a state of spiritual assurance. He, in effect, linked the outer Protestant ritual of revivalism with an inward ritual designed to awaken spiritual sense and set the "Christian Pilgrims" of his time on the road to glory.

By 1840, during the Second Great Awakening, Charles Finney and Asa Mahan had taken the religious values that gave rise to Methodism and expanded on the revival-centered methods articulated by Edwards a century before. What emerged became known as the Oberlin Theology, a successful attempt to reconcile Holiness perfectionism with a more traditional version of a Christian's duty in life. Instead of "sinlessness," the Holy Spirit empowered Christians to work for social reform and, through this effort, hasten the general sanctification of humanity. For Finney, who was the greatest evangelist of his day, the search for social holiness, in the form of justice, was akin to the attainment of perfect love. Thus, abolition, women's rights, and pacifism became key causes within the Finney school of Holiness. The more "this-worldly" focus in Finneyite Christian perfection opened the way for the Keswick movement named after a series of conferences held in England. Keswickians argued that sanctification was a gradual process and that, ultimately, humans could not expect complete sanctification until God initiated the new age (or dispensation) of the Holy Spirit. In any event, though somewhat different in levels of asceticism, all Holiness leaders preached reliance on religious experience as the key determinant of authentic spiritual growth.

In the 1870s, the movement grew in numbers both within Methodism and in other key American denominations such as Congregationalism, Presbyterianism, and various Baptist groups. In part inspired by the teachings of Mrs. Phoebe Palmer, another early prophet in the Holiness saga, the camp meeting came to be the primary institutional structure—the plan—for the spread of Holiness teachings. As many of the mainstream churches became more constrained and more formal, the sectarian impulse created a call for revival. After a particularly successful camp revival meeting held at Vineland, New Jersey, in 1867, the "National Meeting

Association for the Promotion of Holiness" came into existence which, in the years after the Civil War, generated even greater interest and excitement in the Holiness cause.

Again, to return to our "paradox" theme, at the height of the institutional success of the movement, sectarian groups began to break off as members argued over the nature of the Holiness experience and the proper ritual form to express these sometimes overwhelming religious feelings. The more radical elements in the main denominations—particularly in the Methodist church—demanded that true believers "come out" of the dominant institutions and create more spiritually authentic sects. By 1910, these "come-outers" had succeeded in almost totally removing the Holiness movement from the main denominations. Perhaps the most traditional of these untraditional churches is known today as the Church of the Nazarene. We will touch on the history of the Nazarenes in California as the groups developed under the leadership of Phineas F. Bresee. But a much more radical sectarian response began to develop around the turn of the century—the institutional expression of which is the movement we know today as Pentecostalism.

A Short History of Pentecostalism

Pentecostals would have few doctrinal arguments with members of the Holiness movement, or, for that matter, with members of a parent faith be it Methodist, Baptist, or another Christian community holding to conservative, orthodox interpretations of the life and teaching of Jesus Christ. Like the Holiness churches from which they emerged, the Pentecostal churches cling to the notion of sanctification in this life, possess a strict holiness, embrace divine healing, and look with eager expectation to the imminent Second Coming of Christ. What makes Pentecostalism a world unto its own is the insistence on certain types of extraordinary behavior as the measure of spiritual sanctification—in particular, *glossolalia*, or speaking in tongues.

For the Pentecostal believer, all other aspects of religion—doctrines, myths, rituals, symbols, religious institutions, history, tradition—take a back seat to religious experience. Hence, Pentecostalism is a classic sectarian movement, always dividing as new and more profound experiences, *in this life*, are sought. The experience of speaking in tongues, or other spiritual gifts such as healing, prophecy, wisdom (gaining knowledge unattainable by natural means) and discernment of spirits, provides the believer with tangible proof that he or she has been baptized by the Holy Spirit.

Not only is this experiential baptism of the Holy Spirit a sign that the believer is sanctified in the here and now; it also satisfies a classic sectarian need; a need for renewal or return to authentic, apostolic, biblical experience. How does this link Pentecostalism with the biblical past? Tongues, and other spiritual gifts, are seen as a part of the experience of Jesus' disciples at Pentecost, so called because in the second chapter of the Book of Acts, the disciples are gathered on a Jewish holy day, Pentecost. Jewish tradition held that the Law was given on this day, fifty days after Passover. The biblical account tells us that, ". . . suddenly a sound came from heaven like the rush of a mighty wind, and it filled all the house where they were sitting. And there appeared to them [the disciples] tongues of fire, distributed and resting on each one of them. And they were filled with the Holy Spirit and began to speak in other tongues, as the Spirit gave them utterance" (Acts 2: 1-4; RVS). The story goes on to claim that religious leaders from around the world, who had gathered in Jerusalem, became "amazed and perplexed" by the fact that they could understand the disciples, each in his own language. In response to one accusation that the disciples were drunk, Peter, the Apostle, quotes the Old Testament prophet, Joel:

> And in the last days it shall be, God declares, that I will pour out my Spirit upon all flesh, and your sons and your daughters shall prophesy, and your young men shall see visions, and your old men shall dream dreams; yea, and on my menservants and maidservants in those days I will pour out my Spirit; and they shall prophesy. And I will show wonders in the heaven above and signs on the earth beneath, blood, and fire, and vapor of smoke; the sun shall be turned into darkness and the moon to blood, before the day of the Lord comes, the great and manifest day. And it shall be that whoever calls on the name of the Lord shall be saved (Acts 2: 17-21 RSV).

Here we can begin to grasp the intensity of religious experience for the Pentecostal believer. The experience of tongues is an all-encompassing, life changing phenomenon. Not only is it visible evidence of the presence of the Holy Spirit, a testament to sanctification drawn from roots in the Holiness movement, but it turns the focus away from the trials and tribulations of daily life to the imminent coming of a new, spiritual age as predicted in the above biblical passage. The Pentecostal experience also reverberates with each of the four characteristics of sectarian religion mentioned in chapter two. It certainly is millennial in orientation; America will be the place where perfection, the kingdom of heaven, is initiated. Illuminism, or new light from the transcendent realm, can be seen in the availability of the spiritual gifts pouring down from the heavens. All "believers" can participate in salvation by opening up to the Holy Spirit, thus, liberation from bondage is, potentially, a universal blessing. And sanctification, the holiness process of "being perfect as your Father is" finds daily expression in a life of constant spiritual adventure.

To the outsider, tongues may sound like someone speaking, at best, a foreign language that one does not know or, worse, like so much gibberish. But to the Pentecostal convert it is a religious experience that dominates every aspect of daily life. For instance, at the modern, technologically advanced television studies of the Christian Broadcasting Network (CBN), the media center of Pat Robertson's Pentecostal religious organization, a visitor will find one room that serves as the chapel. By no mistake in architecture, it is in the center of the building surrounded by television studies, editing rooms, and production areas. While the rest of the studio is modern in decor, the chapel offers an interior designer's rendition of a first-century Judean place of worship, complete with rustic wooden benches and ancient-looking pottery. At any point in the day, employees of CBN—presumably while on "break"—may be found participating in the religiously intense experience of speaking in tongues. An observer can understand the pejorative use of the label, "holy rollers," to describe Pentecostal worship in that it is unquestionably loud, emotional, free-spirited, and extremely enthusiastic.

Historically, the experience of "tongues" has cropped up at a number of times and in a number of places, including to seventeenth-century French Protestants, eighteenth-century Quakers in England, and even within the more radical, post-Civil War, Holiness groups in the United States. But the roots of the modern Pentecostal movement are found in the work of the Reverend Charles Parham. Again, we find the classic sectarian impulse present in Reverend Parham's spiritual journey. Unable to find authentic religious experience amidst the doctrines and rituals of the Methodist Episcopal Church, Parham left, in 1898, to form a sect in Topeka, Kansas. He called it the Bethel Healing Home. After an extended tour of healing and holiness revivals, he returned to Topeka, in 1900, to found Bethel Bible College.

As the end of the year approached, Parham was busy leading his students through the major tenets of the holiness movement with special emphasis on divine healing and, of course, sanctification. Under Parham's intense direction, students began investigating the baptism of the Holy Spirit, and, upon his return from a short excursion to a nearby revival, he was astonished to find that his students unanimously agreed that "speaking in tongues" was the one and only authentically biblical evidence of baptism with the Holy Spirit.

Convinced that this was, indeed, the proper interpretation of the extraordinary events in the Book of Acts, Parham called for a watchnight service on December 31, 1900. During this service, a precocious student by the name of Agnes Ozman asked Parham to lay hands on her and pray fervently that she be baptized by the Holy Spirit with the assurance of the "tongues" experience. Apparently, shortly after midnight—the first day of the twentieth century—Ozman began speaking in the Chinese language and, according to written accounts by others attending the service, a "halo seemed to surround her head and face." For three days following the experience, she could communicate only in Chinese and, when asked to communicate by writing, she was able to write using only Chinese characters. During a quick succession of prayer vigils throughout the month of January, Parham and his students, all Americans, received the gift of tongues and spoke in twenty-one languages including Spanish, German, Hungarian, Russian, Chinese, Japanese, and Norwegian. This prompted Parham to proclaim that missionary students would no longer have to study foreign languages as preparation for work in other countries. They would simply pray to receive the gift of tongues and, once truly sanctified, could travel the far corners of the globe saving souls in the language of the natives.

Typical of the "paradox" in religious experience, Parham took these uncanny happenings as a sign that he should close the college and set out across the country to spread the Pentecostal message of glory. For Parham, religious institutions belonged to an age that was quickly passing and, in the new dispensation, people would be Christian without the necessity of organizational trappings. One notable revival occurred in Galena, Kansas and lasted four months during the winter of 1903-1904.

In 1905, Parham turned his attention to Texas, and it is here that the California saga begins. When Parham opened a Bible school in Houston, William J. Seymour, an African-American Baptist Holiness preacher, became convinced of his message, left his Baptist sect, and set out for California. As we will see, it was Rev. Seymour who initiated what is, perhaps, the crystallizing event in modern Pentecostal history: the Azusa Street revival of 1906.

The somewhat convoluted sectarian changes within Pentecostalism deserve brief summary, notably its innate tendency for doctrinal disagreements to erupt over the nature of the Pentecostal experience. For instance, members of the Holiness movement, who were Methodist "come-outers," held to the position that "speaking in tongues" was a third blessing after justification and sanctification. Those who came directly to the movement, primarily former Baptists, claimed that any sincere believer could receive the blessing of tongues without the intermediate stage of sanctification. They insisted on but two experiences: justification and the baptism of the Holy Spirit. In fact, today's largest Pentecostal group, the Assemblies of God, dissents from the third blessing doctrine.

A third experiential/doctrinal disagreement erupted over the standard Christian doctrine of the Trinity. A group of ministers began to preach a "Jesus only" or "Jesus' name" doctrine that claimed biblical basis for what amounts to a unitarianism of the second person. They baptize in Jesus' name only and teach that the three beings of the Trinity—Father, Son, and Holy Spirit—are but three names for the one God, Jesus Christ. Often, one finds the title "Apostolic" attached to "Pentecostal" on the church buildings of this "sect-of-a-sect-of-a-sect." These doctrinal differences, in time, created three major subdivisions in the movement, which, in turn, tended to split into six groups along racial lines.

Lastly, two of the more exotic branches of Pentecostalism are the Snake Handlers and the Latter Rain Movement. Snake Handlers add to the experiential package by insisting that holding poisonous snakes and drinking poison are biblically-based signs (Mark 16: 17-19) of an individual's possession of the Holy Spirit. With the death of some adherents, snake-handling activities have been banned in several states. The Latter Rain Movement, a mid-twentieth-century development, stresses the gifts of healing and prophesy and the practice of laying-on-of-hands to heal or impart spiritual gifts to others. More traditional Pentecostals, if one can use the word traditional to describe any of the sects in the movement, have accused Latter Rain believers of religious fanaticism and scriptural manipulation. For all these differences, however, California, as we shall see, provided the place where the promise of perfection was most suited.

The Holiness Movement in California

As bands of inspired Holiness prophets began to roam the United States in the 1870s, initiating revivals and preaching sanctification, it was inevitable that the lure of a growing population of sinners would draw them to California. As tensions with the Methodist Church intensified, for example, radical Methodists began to form independent churches and, during the 1880s, Hardin Wallace along with evangelist Harry Ashcraft and gospel singer James Jayns began leading Holiness revivals in Los Angeles. The Southern California and Arizona Holiness Association, led by James and Josephine Washburn, developed out of this early evangelical work, but the group remained relatively small due to some rather stringent organizational requirements: all members had to experience sanctification, dress plainly, and abstain from liquor, tobacco, and dancing.

As Los Angeles began to explode into a major urban center, the possibility for Holiness centers increased dramatically. City missions provided an institutional format more suited to Holiness doctrines since the poor and wayward were often more than willing to leap into the experiential joys that were part and parcel of the Second Blessing. During the boom years of 1885-1886, T.P. and Manie Ferguson, buoyed by a successful 1879 revival in Santa Barbara, set up the first of a string of Peniel Missions in Los Angeles. Their afternoon street corner meetings and nightly evangelical revivals spread the Holiness message of Christian perfection, but they never considered their work in a sectarian sense. They saw their mission as an on-going Holiness revival and fully expected participants to join a Protestant church of their choice.

The key prophet in the Southern California story of the Holiness movement is Phineas F. Bresee. A New Yorker by birth, he spent his early adult years roaming the Midwest as a circuit pastor in the Methodist Church, and apparently made quite a name for himself as an inspirational, articulate, and authentic religious leader. Unfortunately, some unwise financial investments left him bankrupt and, in 1883, he moved from Iowa to California. Due to his skills as a preacher, his star soon rose in the frenetic Los Angeles atmosphere which culminated in his appointment to the position of pastor of the First Methodist Church in Los Angeles.

It was not long, however, until the sectarian impulse began to drive a wedge between Bresee and the Methodist establishment. After experiencing sanctification himself in 1884 or 1885, Bresee's church services took on a distinctly Holiness stance with emphasis on enthusiastic revivalism, congregational participation, gospel singing, and the second blessing. This simply added to his popularity, and all went quite well for a time until, in 1892, John Vincent, an anti-Holiness clergyman, was appointed Bishop of the Southern California region. Vincent was intent on undermining Bresee's divergent ministry and did so by assigning him to smaller churches on the outskirts of the city that simply did not generate the financial muscle needed to support a growing evangelical movement. When the charismatic Bresee was refused permission to function as a kind of roving missionary throughout the Southern California bishopric, he resigned from the Methodist ministry in 1894.

This interaction between Vincent and Bresee was being replicated within the Methodist movement all across the nation. The Methodist hierarchy decided that enough was enough and that it was high time to douse the sectarian fires threatening their time-honored institution. However, the crackdown on Holiness prophets and their enthusiastic followers only served to force defrocked Holiness ministers to form their own independent churches. And this is exactly what Bresee did. After joining for a year with the Fergusons at the Peniel Mission, disagreements over whether they should "institutionalize" the Holiness revival by starting a church (the Fergusons said no) led Bresee to join forces with Joseph P. Widney in the fall of 1895. After only three and a half weeks conducting independent services in a rented auditorium, the two ministers were so popular that they organized as the Church of the Nazarene. Again, we must note that it was California that provided the place that created the possibility for the explosion of a "made-in-America" religion, a "new order of things." But Bresee's success is also attributable to a perfect match between a prophet's articulation of the sectarian plan and the spiritual, emotional, and even economic status of his followers.

For instance, Bresee seems to have been able to touch the hearts and souls of both the poor *and* the middle class in Los Angeles. Soon on his own again after Widney decided to return to the Methodist Church in 1898, Bresee focused this ministry on the poor and marginalized who seemed to suffer most in the teeming urban jungle of late nineteenth-century Los Angeles. His tabernacle, held in a plain building, was referred to as the "Glory Barn" and the lack of pretense appealed to the disadvantaged who would otherwise feel alienated by the normal pomp and circumstance displayed by more traditional denominations.

Yet Bresee's clear, unadulterated spiritual call for conversion and sanctification struck a moral chord with former Midwesterners from conservative small town/rural religious backgrounds. They found comfort, assurance, a taste of Midwestern values in his ethical code: prohibitions against dancing, drinking, gambling, and ostentatious dress and adornment. In fact, these hard-working Midwestern immigrants soon attracted some level of wealth, and, with their support, Bresee attracted well-known gospel singers and evangelists and even was able to begin publishing the *Nazarene Messenger* in 1898.

But is was really Bresee's unique spin on the Holiness theology that attracted believers of all types. He had the skill to combine the essential Holiness quest with new ideas, new theologies that were gaining currency in the Californian religio-cultural environment. In fact, there is a decidedly "New Thought" twist to his description of the sanctification experience. For Bresee, sanctification was not an end in itself but rather was the beginning of an exciting evolutionary process for the spiritual seeker. Late nineteenth-, early twentieth-century Californians had a penchant for the "perfection process" in their new-found paradise, and Bresee delineated clear steps in the quest for authentic, satisfying, inspiring Christian spirituality.

To summarize a few of Bresee's more mystical teachings: like Christian Science or New Thought, Jesus was more of an exemplar than a one-time-only savior. Jesus was a person who, more than any other human being, was able to live life in the presence of God. As one grew in sanctification, as one more readily lived in the presence of God, the material world would fall away to be replaced by a new spiritual sense. It was as though the sanctification experience was a first step in the process of theosis—the deification of the worldly, the spiritualization of the material. To be in the Holy Spirit was more than just to be in God; to Bresee, it was to be a manifestation of God's own being expressed in human consciousness.

In essence, Bresee, no doubt due to the intellectual/spiritual climate of California, was able to combine ancient strains of Christian mysticism with Bible-based, Protestantized doctrines and get away with it. At the same time, he was most adept at overcoming the religious dilemma that provides an important theme for this chapter. Distrustful of rigid religious organizations, he saw all church activity—preaching, meetings, worship, prayer, etc.—as having a single purpose: to bring individuals into this spiritualization process. Thus, the institution that he created truly provided a springboard into transcendent reality for its adherents. It is no surprise that after merging with other regional Holiness churches, Phineas Bresee's Church of the Nazarene became the largest Holiness denomination in the nation.

The Pentecostal Movement in California

We left the general history of the Pentecostal movement with W.J. Seymour heading for California. But well before this uneducated, but charismatic African-American prophet crossed the border into the Golden State, California was well on its way to becoming the place most suited for the sectarian explosion we know today as Pentecostalism. By April of 1906, Los Angeles was a thriving metropolis of some 228,298 souls, and, to social observers of the time, it often seemed that each soul carried within it an insatiable need for unusual religious stimulation. Certainly every sect, cult, and denomination in the American pantheon of religiosity was represented in the Los Angeles basin. The "perfection in paradise" drive that had been chugging along since Puritan times shifted into high gear as spiritual pioneers from around the nation emigrated to the land where plans and possibilities became realities and promises.

Of course, Phineas Bresee played no small role in preparing the field for the great Azusa Street revival of 1906. For a decade since the founding of the Church of the Nazarene in 1895, his Holiness revivals continued to attract enthusiastic crowds and, by 1906, there were about a dozen Nazarene congregations spread throughout the Los Angeles area.

The quest for sanctification also appears to have touched other denominations. Joseph Smale, a former pastor of the First Baptist Church, opened a mission called the "First New Testament Church" at Burbank Hall and advertised his organization as "a fellowship for evangelical preaching and teaching and Pentecostal life and service." Together, Bresee and Smale represented a kind of "radical fringe" within the Holiness movement, and, much to the dismay of religious leaders within the more established denominations, the two ministers attracted over one thousand believers on any given Sunday. Tension grew within the Methodist and Baptist denominations as the more innovative pew warmers began to profess the doctrine of the "third blessing."

And this is precisely what happened in the case of Neely Terry. Terry, who was a member of the Negro Second Baptist Church in Los Angeles, had heard of Parham's school in Houston. During a visit to the school she not only befriended Seymour but received the experience of speaking in tongues. Upon her return to Los Angeles, she was shocked to find that her family and close friends had been excommunicated from the church for professing the doctrine of tongues as the sign of sanctification. Undaunted by the rebuff, this small group of sectarians formed what they called a Negro Holiness Mission which was in close association with Bresee's church. In March of 1906, Terry suggested that the group invite the young, spiritually intoxicated gentleman she had befriended in Houston to be pastor of the mission. When Seymour accepted the invitation and arrived in Los Angeles in April of that year, no one could have guessed that religious history was about to be made.

Apparently, Seymour's first ministerial outing met with doctrinal disaster. During his first sermon at the Negro Holiness Mission, he wasted no time in declaring that speaking in tongues was the only way one could be assured of baptism in the Holy Spirit. Members of the church were touched by the forceful clarity of his stand, but a Mrs. Hutchinson, who held the reins of authority in the mission, declared his doctrinal position heretical and proceeded to padlock the door of the mission to keep Seymour out.

Out of a job and out of a place to stay, Seymour was taken in by a Richard Asbury and, in the living room of his home on Bonnie

Brae street, after several days of prayer, Seymour and seven others fell to the floor in spiritual ecstasy, absorbed into the "tongues" experience. The news spread like wildfire. Huge crowds began to gather to hear Seymour preach from a makeshift pulpit on the front porch and hear his wife to be, Jennie Moore, play the piano and sing in what was thought to be Hebrew. Authorities complained of the noise and traffic hazard created by the crowds on this narrow street, so Seymour was forced to seek larger quarters to hold his ongoing revival. Eventually, an abandoned Methodist Church building was found at 312 Azusa Street and despite the broken windows and humble interior, the preacher was in business as crowds flocked to hear his message. A front-page article in the April 18, 1906 edition of the *Los Angeles Times* describes the scene as follows:

> Meetings are held in a tumble-down shack on Azusa Street, near San Pedro Street, and the devotees of the weird doctrine practice the most fanatical rites, preach the wildest theories and work themselves into a state of mad excitement in their peculiar zeal. Colored people and a sprinkling of whites compose the congregation, and night is made hideous in the neighborhood by the howlings of the worshipers, who spend hours swaying forth and back in a nerve-racking attitude of prayer and supplication. They claim to have the "gift of tongues" and to be able to comprehend the babel.

Certainly the excitement of the revival coupled with Seymour's charisma and the fact that thousands were experiencing "tongues" would have been enough to qualify this event as significant in American religious history. But another event occurred on April 18, 1906 that propelled the Azusa Street revival to a new level of religious phenomena—and, at the same time, provided a foundation from which Pentecostalism would grew into a bona fide new religious movement. We are speaking of the Great San Francisco Earthquake of 1906.

Apparently, one of the frenzied members of the revival received a vision the day before the quake that prophesied awful destruction to Los Angeles if its citizens did not accept the "tenets of the new faith." The fact that it happened 600 miles to the north did not seem to dull the prophesy, and the geological tremors set off a spiritual earthquake on Azusa Street that would go on for three years. Thousands began to flock to the revival from all over the nation and the world. Major newspapers regularly reported on the event. But the primary impact of the events on Azusa Street—a perfect confluence of prophet, promise, plan, possibility and place—was the creation of a "new order of things"—Pentecostalism—that would spread throughout the United States and to countries as diverse and distant as Sweden, England, India, and Chile. Today, Pentecostalism is one of the most rapidly growing religious sects in the world.

SOURCES AND FURTHER READINGS

Ahlstrom, Sydney E. *A Religious History of the American People*. Garden City, NJ: Doubleday and Co., 1975, 2 Vols.

Albanese, Catherine L. *America: Religions and Religion*. Belmont, CA: Wadsworth Publishing Co., 1981.

Frankiel, Sandra. *California's Spiritual Frontiers: Religious Alternatives in Anglo-Protestantism, 1850-1910*. Berkeley: University of California Press, 1988.

Helm, Thomas E. *The Christian Religion: An Introduction*. Englewood Cliffs, NJ: Prentice Hall, 1991.

Marsden, George. *Fundamentalism and American Culture*. New York: Oxford University Press, 1980.

Melton, J. Gordon. *The Encyclopedia of American Religions*, 3rd ed. Detroit: Gale Research, 1989.

Synan, Vinson. *The Holiness-Pentecostal Movement in the United States*. Grand Rapids, Mich: William B. Eerdmans Publishing Co., 1971.

8 A New Order of Things In a New World Order: International Perspectives on Christian Sectarianism

In this volume we have recounted the California odysseys of a variety of "made-in-America" Christian sects. In doing so our goal has not only been to present an interesting and oft-times neglected facet of California's history, but we have also hoped to convey something of the importance of the study of religion for understanding the modern world in general. As we mentioned in the introduction, religion, whether formal or informal, is a constant in human life. No matter how "secular" the world becomes, human beings will always seek transcendent systems which provide them with meaning and purpose and which offer them guidelines for their behavior. Although here we have emphasized religion in the United States and specifically California, we have tried to convey something of the fundamental importance of religion for every culture.

Thus, just as the study of religion is important for understanding how California developed into the society it is today, so will the study of religion on a global scale be important for understanding the coming global society as it emerges. Today, as major socio-political changes occur in every corner of the planet, we can assume that many of the old religious options will no longer be able to address adequately the new challenges posed by the "new world order." We can also assume that many people will seek new religious options in the hope that these will lift them out of the confusion generated by the rapid changes of the last few years. New prophets will arise, new promises will be made, and new, globally-oriented plans will be touted.

And yet, on the other hand, the new world order could just as well prove to be a unique opportunity for some of the old religious options to catch on globally. Given the advances in communications and travel, we can also look forward to more and more local religious systems breaking free of their hitherto restricted geographical and cultural boundaries and beginning to wield significant influence on the international stage. Already, four of the Christian sects we have been studying in this volume—Mormonism, Seventh-Day Adventism, the Jehovah's Witnesses, and Pentecostalism—have had major successes in establishing themselves beyond the borders of the United States.

Mormonism is probably the sect most successful in transcending its national boundaries. Now one of the fastest growing religions in the world, Mormonism is being touted by many religious historians as quite possibly the next great world religion. From being just one more sectarian option among many such options to have emerged from the "burned-over district" in upstate New York in the early part of the nineteenth century, the Church of Jesus Christ of Latter-Day Saints has, in less than 150 years, grown into a global church of more than 7 million members. This, of course, was no accident. Shortly after the close of World War II, the leadership of the LDS Church decided to make international growth a dominant theme. They saw the postwar period as an opportunity to fulfill the commandment handed down from their martyred founder, Joseph Smith: "Missionize so that the kingdom may become a great mountain and fill the whole earth."

The Church's efforts have paid off. In 1950, the Church had only 180 "stakes" (an ecclesiastical division comparable to a diocese in the Catholic Church), of which close to 90 were in the home state of Utah alone. Today, the Mormons claim 1,700 stakes, of which fewer than one-fourth are in Utah. In 1950, less than 8 percent of the membership resided outside the United States and Canada; today, more than 35 percent do. Growth has been remarkably strong in Latin America, where membership now stands at 2.2 million, a full 29 percent of the Church's members. Moreover, since 1978 and the full acceptance of Blacks into the Church, the Mormons have been expanding rapidly in Africa, especially in Ghana and Nigeria.

Mormons have also been successful in gaining converts in perhaps one of the most challenging mission fields today: the former Soviet Union and Eastern Bloc countries. It has been reported that, as of 1991, the Mormons had 600 to 700 active members in the former Soviet Union. Today, there even stands a Mormon temple at the foot of Mt. Ararat in Soviet Armenia.

Throughout Eastern Europe Mormon missionary activities have been well-financed, well-planned and quite sophisticated, appealing to both the former communist elite as well as to the proletariat of these societies. Proselytization, however, began well before the breakup of the Soviet Union and the collapse of communism. Even before the Berlin Wall fell, the Mormons had missionaries ministering to Eastern European refugees who were then streaming into Vienna. The Mormon cause in Europe has also been helped by members in high places; in 1981, for example, the ambassador to Poland, David Kennedy, himself a Mormon, helped to gain official recognition for the Latter-Day Saints in that country. This, in a country that was under communist rule and still remained overwhelmingly Catholic, was no small achievement.

Although overseas expansion has been a goal of all the sects we have studied in this volume, not all sects have been completely comfortable with it when it happened, especially when such growth was perceived as occurring too fast. Take, for example, the Seventh-Day Adventists. Today, Seventh-Day Adventism operates in 190 countries and its worldwide membership stands at approximately 3.5 million. In the period after World War II, the SDA saw its best growth overseas. Whereas by the 1960s the Church was growing at a rate of 2 to 3 percent annually in America, it was growing at a rate of 5.5 to 6.5 percent overseas. Indeed, by the mid-1980s, a full 76 percent of the 3.5 million Adventists lived in the Third World, while North America had only 16 percent and Europe 6 percent; Australia and New Zealand accounted for another 1 percent.

The shift in the "center of gravity" of Seventh-Day Adventism from America to the Third World was apparent as early as the 1920s. Nevertheless, many in the church hierarchy viewed this situation with some trepidation. One of the problems with such large international growth so early was that the SDA leadership was not prepared for the conversion of the church from a predominantly American institution to an international one. The American power center, unable to see the future in global terms, found it difficult to give up control to foreign leaders. One scholar of Adventism wrote, "The patterns and traditions of the past were hard to break: Seventh-Day Adventism was still largely operated by Americans and according to American perspectives."

Unfortunately, such was the case right up until the 1960s and 70s. Perhaps as a backlash to increasing foreign influence over church policy, American Seventh-Day Adventists became increasingly unwilling to support their overseas missions. Without the American branch playing the cohesive role as it had in the past, the SDA by the late seventies was in danger of breaking into regionally autonomous branches. And despite the fact that a Commission on Church Unity was formed in 1977, the problem remains a pressing one for the Seventh-Day Adventists to this day.

The Jehovah's Witnesses also began to expand considerably overseas in the middle decades of this century, and, since World War II, the growth of the Witnesses internationally has mirrored their phenomenal growth in the United States. Perhaps due to the autocratic structure of the church, the leadership problem has not been much of an issue. Today the Witnesses are active in over 66,000 congregations worldwide. Although membership statistics are hard to come by, current Witness literature reports that "by the end of 1985, more than 3 million Jehovah's Witnesses were sharing preaching work in more than 200 countries." Witnesses also claim that, again in 1985, close to 8 million people attended the Memorial of Christ's death, the most important annual Witness celebration.

Adventists that they are, the Witnesses have always seen the proclamation of the word of God to all the world as a necessary precursor to—indeed the trigger for—the Last Days. Thus, since 1920, the Watchtower Society has produced millions of Bibles, books, magazines, and pamphlets in over 200 languages for worldwide distribution. Recently the Witnesses have had the most success in attracting new members in Latin America, although its early overseas expansion was mostly in Europe, especially in Eastern Europe and the Soviet Union. By the late 1930s, there were more than 2,000 Witnesses in Romania, 1,000 in Poland and hundreds in Czechoslovakia and Hungary. By 1946, more than 4,000 Witnesses were preaching in the Soviet Union—and this despite the fact that all religion was officially proscribed there under severe penalties. It is due to the fact that a fairly large nucleus managed tenaciously to survive underground in these countries that the Witnesses were so prepared to take advantage so quickly of the fall of communism. In 1991, the Jehovah's Witnesses held over thirty large outdoor conventions in Czechoslovakia, Hungary, Yugoslavia, Poland, Romania, and the former Soviet Union. Witness literature claims that such conventions gained 18,293 new converts. The Jehovah's Witnesses is by far one of the fastest growing Christian sects in Eastern Europe.

Although a relative latecomer to the world stage, American Pentecostalism has also been exceedingly successful in the quest for new converts. In Latin America alone, where more than 40 million people are now Protestants, three out of every five of those Protestants are Pentecostals. What's most impressive about this statistic is that the majority of these new Pentecostal converts has been gained in the last ten years. One British scholar of religion, David Martin, suggests that Pentecostalism, a North American "periphery religion," is succeeding so spectacularly in Latin America that it may one day form the "culture core" there, just as Puritanism, once a peripheral religion in England, came to be the culture core of the United States.

Indeed, sometimes proselytization efforts succeed beyond anyone's wildest expectations. Such was the case of Gospel Outreach and its career in Guatemala. Perhaps one of the most interesting Pentecostal groups operating in Latin America, Gospel Outreach has its roots in California. Based in the north of the state, in Eureka, it was founded by a former member of the Assemblies of God, the Reverend Jim Durkin. Since its inception in the early 1970s, Gospel Outreach has always focused on expansion in Latin America. In 1976, the sect started relief operations in Guatemala soon after that country was devastated by a tremendous earthquake. Shortly thereafter, a congregation had established itself in Guatemala City under the name of the Word Church, attracting many Guatemalans of all classes hungering to experience the Holy Spirit.

Suddenly, on March 23, 1982, Gospel Outreach was thrust into the international limelight when one of their members, the retired army general, Efraín Ríos Montt, ascended to the presidency of Guatemala in an army coup d'état. Called by one writer the world's first "born-again dictator," Montt quickly promised a "moral regeneration" of his country. Montt was followed into office by two church elders to serve as his advisors, and every Sunday, Montt would preach to the nation about its moral failings and the efficacy of the Holy Spirit. Word Church officials privately hoped that this was to be the beginning of the evangelization of all of Latin America. This was not to be, however, at least under the leadership of Ríos Montt; citing his general ineffectiveness and "religious fanaticism," the general was removed by another army coup eighteen months later.

Despite this setback however, Pentecostalism continues to grow in Guatemala, and Pentecostals are still vying for political power there. Indeed, in 1985 a Pentecostal candidate won 14 percent of the popular presidential vote. Considering the fact that it is projected that Guatemala will have a Protestant majority by the late 1990s, it is not inconceivable that at some point in the near future another Pentecostal may again gain—and hold—the presidency of this country.

Why have these Christian sects had so much success overseas? Perhaps it is because our sectarian religions have an advantage in this new world order: they have already had the experience of successfully establishing themselves in the pluralistic environment of California. The lessons learned here, we might suppose, probably play a large role in the continuing success of these sects in the rest of the world.

As we have stressed in this volume, California society has always been a microcosm, first of the nation and now of the world. From the beginning, Californians, although Protestant in their religious roots, tended to be unchurched, thus presaging an important characteristic of modern secular society: the lack of binding ties to an inherited denomination. This does not mean, of course, that Californians tended to be less religious than other Americans; on the contrary, Californians have tended to be more ardent in their search for religious options. Californians have always had a penchant for cultural experimentation. They have had a "seeker" spirit, and thus there is a relative tolerance for new lifestyles not found in many areas of the nation. Indeed, it is for this reason that almost all of the Christian sectarian groups we have studied in this volume found a congenial home in California.

It is for this reason as well that, ever since the beginning of the American period, immigrants from around the globe have found California a congenial place to settle. As mentioned above, the great city of San Francisco, for example, actually developed as a city of foreign immigrants. By 1880, 60 percent of its population was either foreign-born or children of foreign-born parents. Relationships between different immigrant groups played a major role in every level of the city's growth and development: politics, economics, culture, and, of course, religion. And to the south, despite the fact that modern Los Angeles was founded by a Midwestern Protestant elite, the cultural hegemony of this group began to slip well before the Second World War. Today, Los Angeles is one of the most ethnically and religiously diverse cities in the world. In addition to Christianity, California as a whole has played host to significant populations of all the world's religions: Judaism, Islam, Hinduism, Sikhism, Buddhism, and many more.

Both of these factors—relative tolerance and mass immigration—have made California a truly pluralistic environment—a place where worldviews not only coexist in relative harmony, but also a place where there is intense competition between religious groups for the recruitment of new members. Only when religious groups have understood the dynamics inherent in this situation did they understand the key to success in the state. Thus, we can imagine that the proselytization experience in California could only have had a profound effect on our sectarian groups as they approached expansion overseas.

As evidence of this effect, we again turn to the Mormons. Today, as mentioned, there are over 700,000 Mormons in California; beautiful temples have been built in Los Angeles, San Diego, and Oakland, and Mormonism has become a vibrant and influential force in many communities. Most importantly, however, out of the Mormon's California experience has arisen a new Mormon model for proselytization. This new model for church growth arose directly out of the uniquely Californian multicultural, urban experience. After the initial years of persecution in the nineteenth century, Mormons adroitly went about the business of articulating their worldview in then-prevailing American values; values that, over the past generation, have now come under attack. We are speaking here of sexist, racist attitudes that, for practically the first 175 years of the nation, had made the quintessential American experience a privileged one for white, male citizens.

In many ways, therefore, as the Salt Lake Mormon community grew and prospered, Mormons outdid other conservative enclaves in maintaining white supremacy in the social environment of Utah. In fact, this old, predominantly white image of Mormonism included doctrinally-authorized racism. Up until 1978, people of African-American descent were not permitted in the priesthood since it was believed that blacks were descendants of Ham, the second son of Noah, who was cursed in the Genesis account.

For generations, the racist tendencies in the Mormon Church fit nicely with the general racism in American society, which thus allowed the unabated growth of Mormonism over the course of the past 150 years. But attitudes that generated success in the United States through the 1950s will not work in the global arena of the late twentieth century. What the California church is providing is, indeed, a global model which reflects the attempt by the church, at large, to transform itself from a traditionally white, Anglo-Saxon, American sect to a world religion.

Today, the church is finding its largest growth in Asia, Central America, and Africa, and it is the California stakes where the programs that facilitate the new proselytizing effort were developed. For instance, the Pasadena stake, with roots back to the earliest Mormon settlers, has worked hard to generate a multicultural atmosphere along with support systems for the ever-expanding middle-class community of non-whites which characterizes the demographics of the Los Angeles basin. Spanish-speaking branches and services in Chinese are common. Classes in English as a Second Language are offered. Mormon emphasis on family values appeals to a population that is seriously threatened by the breakdown of the nuclear family. In fact, it is estimated that the population of the Mormon Church in Southern California is at least 20 percent non-white. Because of the conversion of non-whites and a new openness to diversity, the California church more accurately reflects the multiculturalism of the world as a whole.

All of this, of course, raises is few eyebrows back in Utah; but, somewhere in the Mormon heavens, Samuel Brannan must be smiling, knowing that if the place called Zion is to be the entire world, it is the Californians who now have the plan and, in their embrace of multiculturalism, have opened up the possibility for its realization. *Mutatis mutandis*, this could well be the most important lesson learned by all our Christian sects from their sojourn in the Golden State.

SOURCES AND FURTHER READING

Land, Gary (ed.) *Adventism in America*. Grand Rapids, Mich.: Wm. B. Eerdmans Publishing Co., 1986.

Ludlow, Daniel H. (ed.) *Encyclopedia of Mormonism*. New York: Macmillian Publishing Co., 1992.

Martin, David. *Tongues of Fire: The Explosion of Penetecostalism in Latin America*. London: Basil Blackwell, 1990.

Maxwell, Joe. "New Kingdoms for the Cults" in *Christianity Today*, January 13, 1992. Vol 36: 1, pp. 37-40.

Stoll, David. *Is Latin America Turning Protestant?* Berkeley: University of California Press, 1990.

Bibliography

Albanese, Catherine L. *America: Religions and Religion.* Belmont, CA: Wadsworth Publishing Co., 1981.

Ahlstrom, Sydney E. *A Religious History of the American People.* Garden City, NY: Doubleday and Co., 1975. 2 Vols.

Bailey, Paul. "The Church of Jesus Christ of Latter Day Saints" in *The Religious Heritage of Southern California: A Bicentennial Survey*, ed., Francis J. Weber. Los Angeles: Interreligious Council, 1976.

Bishop, Guy M. "'We Are Rather Weaker in Righteousness Than in Numbers'; The Mormon Colony at San Bernardino, California, 1851–1857" in *Religion and Society in the American West*, eds. Carl Guraneri and David Alvarez. Lanham, MD: University Press of America, 1987.

Braden, Charles S. *Christian Science Today: Power, Policy, Practice.* Dallas: SMU Press, 1989.

___. *Spirits in Rebellion.* Dallas: SMU Press, 1963.

Frankiel, Sandra Sizer. *California's Spiritual Frontiers: Religious Alternatives in Anglo-Protestantism, 1850-1910.* Berkeley: University of California Press, 1988.

Gottschalk, Stephen. *The Emergence of Christian Science in American Religious Life.* Berkeley: University of California Press, 1973.

Guraneri, Carl, and Alvarez, David, (eds.). *Religion and Society in the American West.* Lanham, MD: University Press of America, 1987.

Helm, Thomas E. *The Christian Religion: An Introduction.* Englewood Cliffs, NJ: Prentice Hall, 1991.

Hine, Robert V. *California's Utopian Colonies.* San Marino, CA.: The Huntington Library, 1953.

Judah, J. Stillson. *The History and Philosophy of the Metaphysical Movements in America.* Philadelphia: Westminster Press, 1967.

Klimo, Jon. *Channeling: Investigations on Receiving Information from Paranormal Sources.* Los Angeles: Jeremy P. Tarcher, Inc., 1987.

Kotkin, Joel. "Mission from Utah" in *California Magazine.* July, 1991.

Land, Gary (ed.) *Adventism in America.* Grand Rapids. MI: Wm. B. Eerdmans Publishing Co., 1986.

Ludlow, Daniel H. (ed.) *Encyclopedia of Mormonism.* New York: Macmillian Publishing Co., 1992.

McLoughlin, William G. *Revivals, Awakenings, and Reform.* Chicago: University of Chicago Press, 1978.

McWilliams, Carey. *Southern California: An Island on the Land.* Salt Lake City: Peregrine Books, 1983.

Marsden, George. *Fundamentalism and American Culture.* New York: Oxford University Press, 1980.

Martin, David. *Tongues of Fire: The Explosion of Penetecostalism in Latin America.* London: Basil Blackwell, 1990.

Maxwell, Joe. "New Kingdoms for the Cults" in *Christianity Today*, January 13, 1992. Vol. 36: 1, pp. 37-40.

Melton, J. Gordon. *The Encyclopedia of American Religions*, 3rd Ed. Detroit: Gale Research, 1989.

McGuire, Meredith. *Religion: The Social Context.* Belmont, CA: Wadsworth Press, 1981.

Moore, Laurence R. *In Search of White Crows: Spiritualism, Parapsychology, and American Culture.* New York: Oxford University Press, 1977.

Schneider, Herbert W., and Lawton, George. *A Prophet and a Pilgrim: Being the Incredible History of Thomas Lake Harris and Laurence Oliphant; Their Sexual Mysticisms and Utopian Communities Amply Documented to Confound the Skeptic.* New York: Columbia University Press, 1942.

Simmons, John K. *The Ascension of Annie Rix Militz and the Home(s) of Truth: Perfection Meets Paradise in Early 20th Century Los Angeles,* unpublished dissertation, 1987.

Singleton, Gregory. *Religion in the City of Angeles: American Protestant Culture and Urbanization, Los Angeles, 1850-1930.* Ann Arbor: UMI Research Press, 1979.

Stark, Rodney, and Bainbridge, William. *The Future of Religion.* Berkeley, CA: University of California Press, 1985.

Stoll, David. *Is Latin America Turning Protestant?* Berkeley: University of California Press, 1990.

Synan, Vinson. *The Holiness-Pentecostal Movement in the United States.* Grand Rapids, Mich: William B. Eerdmans Publishing Co., 1971.

Weber, Francis J. (ed.). *The Religious Heritage of Southern California: A Bicentennial Survey.* Los Angeles: Interreligious Council, 1976.

Index

DATE DUE